SOCIO-LINGUISTIC CONSTRAINTS IN TEACHING ENGLISH

About the Author

Pratibha Gupta is a faculty member of University Department of English, L.N. Mithila University, Darbhanga. She is visiting resource person in Teacher's Training Programmes conducted by CIEFL & SCERT Patna.
She did her Ph.D. in ELT and had a number of publications in national and international journals of repute. She had conducted research project in psycholinguistics. Her research interests include ELT, socio-linguistics and psycholinguistics. She is associated with SEMAT and SCERT Patna in projects of teaching material preparation in English and Sarva Shiksha Abhiyan.

SOCIO-LINGUISTIC CONSTRAINTS IN TEACHING ENGLISH

PRATIBHA GUPTA
Department of English
L.N. Mithila University, Darbhanga

CONCEPT PUBLISHING COMPANY, NEW DELHI-110059

ISBN 81-8069-060-1

First Published 2004

Published and Printed by
Ashok Kumar Mittal
Concept Publishing Company
A/15-16, Commercial Block, Mohan Garden
NEW DELHI-110059 (India)

Phones : 25351460, 25351794
Fax : 091-11-25357103
Email : publishing@conceptpub.com

DEDICATED TO MY PARENTS
WHO
CANDLED THE LIGHT OF WISDOM IN ME

Preface

In preparing this book, my aim is to satisfy the needs of the university students of ELT and trainee teachers who require the comprehensiveness of the original work but not its theoretical discussion or wealth of exemplification. This is a modified version of my research work in Maithili speech community. It was undertaken to examine the status, role and ELT situation in Maithili Speech community. It views ELT situation of the study area with inter-cultural perspective. In second language acquisition, an individual from one socio-linguistic community is concerned with adopting symbolic representation of another socio-linguistic community. It involves not only individuals but also their language and culture.

When language teaching is taken as a means of communication and interaction, it is necessary to provide a detail profile of the context in which the language is used. To develop an understanding of language in context is a prerequisite for better performance. Learning a language, as it is spoken by a particular group is learning the shared meanings, values and practices of that group, as they are embodied in the language.

An individual's life pattern, attitudes, creeds, religion even most of his worldview are shaped largely by his environment where he dwells. He is influenced by family, community, country and even by language. No culture is composed of clones and is fashioned by the pervading prevailing tenets. When a person who has nurtured by one culture is placed in juxtaposition with another, his reaction may be of curiosity, entrenchment, frustration, repulsion or confusion. Such a predicament may be very threatening and until the threat is understood and removed language learning my be blocked.

It is the responsibility of foreign/second language teachers to recognise the trauma their students experience. To assist them they must be aware of the cultural issues involved in the learning process along with pedagogical and non-pedagogical tenets. These are invisible factors but ignorance of these factors very often resulted in hackneyed and poor language learning. Learners must be brought to the point where these cultural and non-pedagogical factors becomes an aid to language learning rather than a hindrance.

PRATIBHA GUPTA

Acknowledgements

I wish to acknowledge my deep sense of gratitude to my revered teacher Prof. S.N. Palit, ex-Head, P.G. Department of English, L.N. Mithila University, Darbhanga for his inspiring and ungrudging help and guidance.

I am extremely grateful to Dr. D. Kanak Durga, Department of English, Arts College, Osmania University, Hyderabad; Prof. A.K. Sharma, Sultan Qaboos University, Mascot; and Prof. A. Jha, Head, Department of English, L.N. Mithila University for their valuable and constructive suggestions.

I am also grateful to all those persons who are directly or indirectly involved with the completion of this book. I am thankful to all those writers for the references appearing in this book.

My special thanks are to Prof. B. Thakur, Vice-Chancellor, L.N. Mithila University and his wife for their inspiration and help. I owe a special debt to Prof. S.S.N. Sinha for his unified guidance.

Finally, I express my gratitude to my husband Dr. A.K. Gupta and my sons Gautam and Gaurav for their sustained support and encouragement. I owe my special thanks to Mr. Ashok K. Mittal for publishing this book.

Pratibha Gupta

CONTENTS

Preface vii
Acknowledgements viii
Abbreviations xi

1. Study of Existing Situation **13**
Introduction 13
A Geographical and Historical Outline 13
Current Use of English 14
Indian English 15
Government Policies following Independence 16
After Effect of Government Policy 16
Major Approaches to Area-centred ELT Research 17
Darbhanga as a Socio-linguistic Area 20
Theoretical Concept behind the Study 21
Theoretical and Methodological Framework and its Goal 26

2. Conventional English Teaching Methodology: Premisses and Practices **28**
Introduction 28
Conventional English Teaching and its Variables 29
Teachers 29
Students 34
Policy Making Design for Education and Syllabus 40
Materials and Teaching Aids
Methodology 55
Evaluation and Testing 91
Requirements of Good Examination and Test Procedures 99
Issues in Communicative Testing 104
Socio-cultural Variables 111
Guardian, Society and Non-linguistic Factors 112

3. Socio-Cultural Aspects of ELT Theories of Nativisation and its Function **114**
Introduction 114
Basic Socio-linguistic Concept 116
Speech Community and Speech Fellowship 116

Linguistic Repertoire 117
Range and Depth 118
Communicative Competence 119
Deviations, Errors and Mistakes 119
Position of English in the Post-Colonial Era 120
Nativisation in Darbhanga 125
The Acrolect 126
The Mesolect 126
The Basilect 127
Context of Culture 127
Context of Situation
Effects of Culture and Deviations from the Norm 134
Syntax 138
Lexis 143

4. Analysis of the Data **148**
Technicalia 148
Schools — All are Inter-Schools 148
Colleges 149
Collection of Data 149

5. Assessment and Observation **161**
Introduction 161
Assessment 161
Conclusion 170

6 Conclusion with Remedial Suggestions **172**
Introduction 172
Summary 172
Implication for Applied Linguistics 175
Language Planning 176
Teaching English as a Non-native Language 176
Suggestions for Remedial Measures 177
Scope of Further Research 180

Apendices
Appendix A: Samples of Language Laboratory 181
Appendix B: Samples of Intermediate Question and Answer Scripts 183
Appendix B_2: Intermediate Answer Script 195
Appendix C : Questionnaire for Students and Teachers 199

Bibliography 206

Index 223

Abbreviations

AE	—	American English
BA	—	Bachelor of Arts
BBC	—	British Broadcasting Corporation
BE	—	British English
CNP	—	Communication Need Processor
DTB	—	Desired Terminal Behaviour
EB	—	Entrance Behaviour
EFL	—	English as a Foreign Language
ELT	—	English Language Teaching
ESL	—	English as a Second Language
FL	—	Foreign Language
FLS	—	Foreign Language Speaker
G	—	General
GIE	—	General Indian English
H	—	Honours
IE	—	Indian English
L_1	—	First Language
L_2	—	Second Language
LNMU	—	Lalit Narayan Mithila University
MSE	—	Maithili Speakers of English
MT	—	Mother Tongue
NCERT	—	National Council of Educational Research and Training
NP	—	Need Processor
OUP	—	Oxford University Press
PWE	—	Pass Without English
REG.L.	—	Regional Language
RP	—	Received Pronunciation
S	—	Subsidiary
SAE	—	South Asian English
SALs	—	South Asian Languages
SBE	—	Standard British English
SIE	—	Standard Indian English
SL	—	Second Language
SLS	—	Second Language Speaker
SME	—	Speakers of Maithili English
TV	—	Television
VCP	—	Video Cassette Player

1

Study of Existing Situation

Introduction

Nineteenth and twentieth centuries have witnessed a remarkable popularity in the use of English. This has been caused by the recent political and economic influences of the United States and the increasing use of English as an international language for science and technology, trade, diplomacy and literature. About 400 million people are non-native speakers of English who did not learn English as their first language but have formally studied or acquired it for a variety of purposes.

A Geographical and Historical Outline

India is grouped with the South East Asian countries in matters of English teaching. But it is almost inevitable to note that we are the only people who, as a matter of national policy, were made to learn English at schools for the past century or more. Our compatriots have been learning English as a second language at schools and universities, as one of the most important subjects of study. At first, a selected minority enjoyed the privilege, but these days practically a large number of junior and senior High School pupils study English. English teaching was started in early nineteenth century to suit the needs of the English rulers. Its status and role changed after independence.

Quirk (1981) calculates that the 25 million Indians who regularly use English give India the third largest population of English speakers in the world after the United States and Britain. Kachru (1976) observes that in country like India, "English is used to teach and maintain the indigenous pattern of life and culture, to provide a link in culturally and linguistically pluralistic societies and to maintain a continuity and uniformity in educational, administrative and legal systems."

Current Use of English

Currently English language has a significant continuing role. Durant (1987) has estimated that roughly one-fifth of Indian newspapers and one-third of all books published in India are in English (Kachru 1983). Besides Hindi, English is the only genuinely Pan-Indian language available for use in broadcasting by 'All India Radio' and in the rapidly developing field of Television. The most striking indication of the continuing role of English is the scale of its everyday use. Even the people of lower strata use a large number of English words in their daily use in place of the vernacular words. All these show the deep roots of English in our culture and life. Though these words are phonetically different from the original words and efforts are made to make them sound 'English'. A quite interesting article "बिहार पहुँच कर 'नरभसा' गये शरद जोशी" appeared in *Nav Bharat Times* (9-4-1990). This article shows the deep impact of English on our daily routine. Some of the words are phonetically so distorted that they hardly correspond even to the accepted Indian English (IE) models, regional strains have lent dialectal variety to Indian English.

In India English is used mainly for two purposes : One for international communication in domains of multinational industries, science and technology, commerce and banking, transportation, tourism etc., and as an institutionalised second language for education, government, business and inter-ethnic communication.

An important consequence of the global use of English by non-native speakers (especially Indians) has been that as it is used in new social and cultural contexts and in contact with other languages, English is often "nativised" (Kachru 1918b : 18). That is, in each non-native context of use, new forms and functions of English develop which are systematic and productive in that locale but which would be considered deviant in countries where English is spoken as a native language and the result is very difficult to understand for other listeners who are used to a different set of prosodic signals (Lowenberg 1984).

In contexts where English is used as second language, these non-native varieties of English, Kachru (1985) says, differ systematically from the native speaker varieties at almost all linguistic levels : phonology, morphology, syntax, semantics, style and discourse.

In India English occupies the position of an influential second language but no uniform standard is followed all over the country. The standards in metropolitan cities and areas are quite different from those followed in semi-urban and rural areas.

Indian English

Indian English (IE) denotes "English spoken by one who had learnt at least one Indian language before he started learning English". Durant (1987), observes that English teaching in a multilingual society differs significantly and idiosyncratically from two types of language situations: bilingual speakers of English and speakers for whom English is very much a foreign language and exclusively foreign language learners. The difference between the two kinds of English can be attributed to the early educational background of the speakers. There are Indians who have been educated at public schools whose accent is unquestionably RP, and there are those who may not have been educated in those public schools and do not have the opportunity to learn the standard BE. It is generally agreed that IE as spoken by educated people in India does not differ radically from standard native English in grammar or vocabulary, but phonetically. One of the reasons for the difference is due to first language pull. Mother tongue habits interfere with the target language hence these varieties are quite often named with reference to the first language of their speakers. Choudhary (1989) observes that such educated Indians had not received any systematic training in internationally accepted standard form. A great majority of nearly 23 million speakers of English would belong to this category. "Census Handbook on Mother Tongues in India (1977)" reports the existence of more that 1,500 mother tongues in the country.

There are some phonological differences among different regional varieties of IE. These divergences are due to a number of reasons. Several phonological features typical to IE are common to all the studies undertaken so far. Bansal (1967) has also observed that non-use of weak forms of words in unstressed positions, non-use of short vowels in unstressed syllables, difficulty with word initial and word final, sometimes also with word medial, clusters of consonants, -----

elision of vowels are common to many varieties of IE.

Government Policies following Independence

Since the end of the colonial period, there has always been existed, the constitutional capability to scale down, even completely eradicate, this policy of education through English imposed by earlier, British administrations (Durant 1987:3). But under article 343(2) of the Constitution, English remained the language for all official purposes until 26 January, 1965, then to be replaced by Hindi. During the years, two kinds of pressures were developing in ELT situation in the country. In Kunzru committee (set up to investigate future language planning for the country) report of 1957, arguments were put forward for minimising any contraction in the role of English or English education in India. At the same time this committee proposed two important changes in approaches to English. First, the linking of the study of English literature to the study of Indian literature and second major expansion in the study, at all appropriate levels of linguistics. In early 1960, the committee of experts under G.C. Banerjee also sought to reaffirm a long-term usefulness for English, whilst arguing for modernisation in the subject. That would promote it less as a colonial, cultural inheritance than as instrument of scientific learning. This first kind of pressure from experts and committees may have had only limited circulation and influence, but it drew attention directly to unresolved and partly unexplored issues within English studies of the time. The second kind of pressure came in the form of riots, especially in Tamil Nadu in 1963, in response to the imminent imposition of Hindi in (Southern) territories where the language tended to be seen as a favoured regional, rather than genuinely Pan-Indian language. Largely as a result of these riots and following the Official Language Act of 1967, English joined Hindi as an additional language. Subsequently, this policy of accommodation has been consolidated as the "Three language formula", containing use of Hindi, English as link language and one regional language.

After Effect of Government Policy

Framed by these broad social and historical circumstances, the use of English in India, currently takes place on a scale that suggests for the language a significant continuing role. Besides Hindi, English is the only genuinely Pan Indian language available for use in broadcasting by All India Radio and in the rapidly developing field of television. Moreover, a considerable amount of creative writing in English has established major cultural claims for the language in the sub-continent, quite independently of further contact with the West. The most striking indication of the continuing role of English, on the simple scale of its every day use, approximately Three per cent of all Indians are English using bilinguals, giving the language currency parity. This percentage gains its full impact when projected as actual number of speakers. Three per cent of Indian population means about 20 million people (the equivalent of about one-third of British English speakers, and one-tenth the number of speakers of English in the United States). It is desirable to advance, in addition to the case for communicative skills in learners, the following two further claims for teaching:

(a) That the study of English can help and promote understanding of how the modern identity of India (in language) has emerged from a specific historical development.
(b) That the study of English leads to increased awareness of the particular language which is used as a 'link' language in various spheres of activity and also what inevitable difficulties surround its use in this way.

Major Approaches to Area-centred ELT Research

Research into non-native varieties to date has focused on performance varieties in the country. A list of such studies in recent years on Indian English (presented in alphabetical order) is given below:

Bansal	1969
Das	1982
Kachru	1965, 1966, 1973, 1978, 1983
Mehrotra	1982
Parashar	1979
Verma	1982

Many regional studies focus on the regional varieties. These regional researches show how regional languages cause nativisation of English. In the light of these regional variations a large number of studies focus on almost every aspect of English language teaching. Right from phonology to discourse variations are dealt with change of emphasis. We would refer to these studies which have highlighted nativisation at different levels and area of problem in those social settings. Only those works are listed which, in one way or other, are related to this present study.

V. Saraswathi (1978) analyses core remedial grammar based on error analysis to students of Intermediate. She discusses how effective are our prescribed grammar books and to what extent they help our learners.

S.V. Parashar (1979) discusses aspect of function and forms of Indian English, with reference to socio-linguistics. He deals with social psychology of language. His study covers the use of language in social interaction from a psychological perspective, as well as learner's attitude towards varieties of languages.

M. Kundu (1980) has also tried to find out the socio-linguistic factors which affect English language teaching to the disadvantaged learners of Orissa. The extent of impact of their home environment and their socio-economic condition in learning English has been dealt with in his study.

Sudesh K. Sawhney (1980) has studied the socio-linguistic factors affecting acquisition of English as a second language. He deals with the environment where learners live. Structure of society, general atmosphere, medium of instruction, composition of school and college also affect the teaching learning situation.

Y.P. Yadav (1980) deals with time, tense and aspects of English and Maithili. He presents a contrastive study of the two languages with regard to limited area of time and tense.

Ms. Aroti (1981) explores the use of mother tongue at the undergraduate level in Rajasthan. She tries to explain the extent to which a teacher can use mother tongue in English classroom. It is a sociolinguistic inquiry into the language learning-teaching situations.

S.C. Chaudhary (1981) studied the same problem in relation to the tribal students of Ranchi. He attempts to identify the sociolinguistic correlates of Ranchi University's second year Intermediate tribal students' achievement in learning English.

Bijoy Kumar Lal (1981) inquires about the first language interference in the acquisition of English as third language. It is an exploration of the special problems encountered by the Kondhe tribal students of Orissa in acquiring English.

J.A. Ranjtha (1983) studied the form and function of English as used in classroom. She analyses language in terms of its form and function. She shows how forms and function of a classroom language are different from the discourse used outside classroom.

Y.P. Yadav (1983) studied 'Movement rules in Maithili and English'. He searches implication for the theory of Government and Binding. His area of study is syntax of the language.

Mrs. Lima Manuel (1986) tries to find out factors causing differences in the proficiency level of students entering Intermediate courses. To fill the gap she suggests some material for remedial English teaching.

Ranjit Mukherjee (1986) inquires about teaching paragraph writing through an experience approach. He discusses how methods and techniques can be used for teaching effective paragraph writing.

E. Aruna Satyam (1986) studies psycho-social correlates of comprehension in the second language of adolescent bilinguals.

Julu Sen (1986) examines the syllabus followed in West Bengal regarding oral communication component at plus two level.

G. Sudhakar (1987) studied structuralist grammar and communicative grammar in English classes in regional medium schools.

T.K. Pramanik (1988) studied effective variables related to learning English as a second language at the post-secondary stage in Orissa. He says learning a second language is not merely an intellectual activity, nor it is as postulated by behaviourists, the outcome of habit formation. Because a total physical, intellectual and emotional involvement is necessary to successfully send and interpret linguistic message. Language grows in the culture and bears the imprint of the culture. That is why, problems faced by learners is a kind of language shock. His work discusses student's variables in context of culture.

S.C. Chaudhary (1989) discusses some aspects of the phonology of Indian English with regard to Maithili speakers.

C.J. Thomas (1990) has studied the spoken English of Junior Intermediate students with reference to medium of instruction and the phonetic correlates of 'good' and 'bad' spoken English. He tries to find out those regional factors which affect intelligibility of the language. His concern is mainly with phonetic and suprasegmental features.

Usha Prasad Paruchuri (1992) makes an attempt to characterise classroom interaction and communication in classes of various sizes, including large classes. She reveals that the teachers talk generally related to pedagogical functions, and the amount of interaction relating to genuine communicative purposes was limited in quantity. Therefore, she concludes that it is not the size of class but the nature of input and interaction in the class which is significant in classroom communication.

A.K. Sharma (1992) through the teaching and testing of grammar at intermediate level in Bihar tries to show the effect of different socio-economic variables in the teaching learning situation in specific context of Bihar.

Darbhanga as a Socio-linguistic Area

Darbhanga is situated in North Bihar, surrounded by Samastipur, Sitamarhi, Madhubani, Muzaffarpur and Nepal. These are mostly Maithili spoken areas. Most of the learners coming from these areas belong to middle and lower middle income groups. In the lower middle income group, most of them are first generation learners of English. It is an economically backward area and there is no industry. It has no direct link with other parts of the country, neither has it anything important to attract outsiders. Therefore, it has negligible contact with people from other parts of the country. The city, now the administrative headquarters of Darbhanga division consisting of four revenue districts adjoining the territory of Nepal, was once famous as the seat of the Darbhanga Estate and it has one of the oldest medical colleges and hospital in the state of Bihar. Presently, the erstwhile palaces of the Darbhanga Raj house two universities. There are five Inter-high schools and 15 colleges. The population of the city, the second largest in North Bihar, has thin crust of upper-middle income group, largely consisting of professional people, namely, doctors, lawyers, government officials and businessmen, most of whom send their wards outside the state for education. The dominant language of the area is Maithili, a member of the branch of the Ardha-Magadhi family of language, with distinct phonological and grammatical features. The culture of the people is different and distinctive. Their language, attitude, manner, life style, test, temperament and values make them different from the rest of the state.

The initial linguistic situation of the place also affects the teaching/learning situation. Hindi enjoys the status of the National Language, which unfortunately is not accepted by some other dominant language groups. Bihar is mini-India in the sense that there are many language groups. A large number of languages spoken in the area among which Bhojpuri, Magdhi, Awadhi, Urdu, Maithili are major groups. Darbhanga has a predominance of Maithili speakers. Most of the students have Maithili as their first language or mother tongue. This language is spoken in the northern region of Bihar. Though it is spoken all over Bihar, its maximum impact is seen in and around Darbhanga. It was once considered to be a dialectal variation of Hindi. Maithili speakers' attitude to learn English is not different from the speakers of other parts. They consider it a prestigious language and there is a strong feeling that acquisition of the language ensures social prestige and even professional competence.

The ELT situation in Darbhanga provides an interesting case for a micro-level study of ELT situation in Darbhanga.

Theoretical Concept behind the Study

Earlier studies done in the area of English language teaching highlighted different aspects of language learning in various socio-cultural settings. It is a well-known fact that in the matter of culture and language, India has a diversified setting. These socio-cultural background affects teaching/learning situation. In the socio-cultural background of Darbhanga no extensive work has been done. Though there are three works based on investigation of correlation between Maithili and English which are mentioned above. The present study is different in its approach. It highlights the impact of socio-cultural factors on the teaching-learning situation of students studying in and around Darbhanga. It tries to find out pragmatic and functional approaches for interpreting the factors affecting the intelligibility and teaching/learning situation of language (English) and the first language pull on Intermediate students.

When we come to consider the sub-standard and pidginised forms of English, which are in widespread use, the sub-standard and pidginised forms are clearly unacceptable and must simply be called wrong. Therefore, throughout it is tried to show what does happen rather than what should happen. Forms and expressions of the substandard type need to be corrected if the speaker wishes to speak English which is intelligible and accepted on an international scale.

Nativised features of these speakers' English, from phonology to creative literary styles, has to be analysed in conjunction with the sociolinguistic contexts in which these forms are used. It is observed that regardless of overall proficiency in English, every speaker of this variety employs nativised feature variably according to norms of socio-linguistic appropriateness.

In the course of coaching my sons and teaching my students at N.J. Mahila College, Laheriasarai, I found a wide gap in terms of performance in the use of English between an average learner of this area and that of one who follows almost the same course in a school outside the state. It aroused my interest in ELT situations. In general, every parent discusses the deteriorating condition of teaching/learning situation. Even the people of lower strata are becoming aware of the importance of English. The fall-out was the numerous English Medium Public Schools, at least one in every ward of the city. Besides these public schools, there are a good number of coaching institutions and centres for spoken English courses. But in spite of this positive attitude of people towards English and large number of schools, the condition of English teaching and learning has deteriorated further. The proficiency level of the students and workable knowledge of the language is very poor despite the motivation of the learners and their parents.

The teaching in schools and colleges has become stereotyped and examination oriented. One interesting phenomenon is the fatal loss of credibility of school, college teaching programmes largely due to the general falling standards, adherence to old and outworn teaching methodology, extensive use of spurious text materials and 'guides', frequent interruptions of teaching schedules by strikes and boycotts resorted to by the teaching and non-teaching staff, the general climate of apathy and indifference to the avowed objective of teaching/learning and finally the collapse of examination/evaluation system. The situation is being exploited by the so-called public schools and coaching centres, resulting in heavy absenteeism from schools and colleges. There is also a large scale exodus of students to other states in search of excellence.

From the survey and personal interviews (*See* Chapter 4 and 5), it becomes obvious that our learners study English for its functional use. They use the language in some restricted domains. Tables 7, 8, 9 and 10 in Chapter 4 show most of them want to use the language either for cultivating language skill or for occupational purpose. For enjoyment, entertainment, they avoid the English language and prefer to use their mother tongue on informal and personal levels. At present, they need the language for purely educational purpose such as comprehension, reading skills, note-making, note-taking or speaking in formal situations. They are also keenly aware of the value of the competence of these kills in building up a prosperous career. But at the available model of teaching/learning English, they reap frustration and despondency. This awareness is a new trait and must be taken into consideration for bringing about a qualitative change in ELT programme offered in schools and colleges.

Bihar had suffered a setback in the matter of teaching/learning of English when its status as a compulsory subject in school and college curricula was changed in 1967 by making it an optional subject of studies at college level and the provision of PWE (Pass Without English) Division in the school final examinations. Very recently, the Chief Minister of Bihar has shocked his own partymen, who were committed to the abolition of the use of English at all levels, by openly coming out in favour of re-introducing English as a compulsory subject from the primary level of education. Though the legislation proposed by him could not be formalised under pressure from his own party, he has made public statements to the effect that for the uplift of the socially and economically backward castes, exposure to English is an urgent necessity. This sudden development after a lapse of nearly 25 years of official hostility to English represents a wind of change. This may be the right moment to understand and evaluate the ELT situation in the state of Bihar in general and in socially and economically backward and poor region like Darbhanga in particular, to take advantage of the favourable wind and to make the ELT programme an effective tool for the attainment of the desired goal.

Syllabus in state level systems all over India have, in their essential framework, remained unchanged for more than three decades. M.L. Tickoo (1992) asserts that the syllabus (with the increasing demand of English and awareness for its functional aspect) needs modification. Though the syllabus framed for the Intermediate students is highly ambitious, its implementation in text books and in the classroom presentation is very unsatisfactory. There is no indication for its effective implementation. There appears to be a very big gap between theory and practice owing largely to continuing emphasis on doing well at the end of the term examination as the primary goal of the programme.

Teaching materials (text books) are manifestations of syllabus. The topics are taken from varied situations but they are presented as set pieces for the development of language skills. However, in the classroom presentation these objectives are ignored and the language content is not given due importance. The teaching is content oriented in the form of summary of the pieces. Explanatory passages are also set to evaluate the level of comprehension of the ideas, thought and feelings in specific passages. These situations described are quite unfamiliar to our students. Due to its low price, the getup and presentation are of poor quality. It lacks illustrations and exercise materials.

Teaching methods and techniques used are age old. Most of the time lecture method is used in which teacher delivers lectures and students listen to them passively. The methods and techniques adopted do not demand students' participation. Very few of them participate actively. Other reasons are time-pressure, load of syllabus, emphasis on finishing syllabus, etc. These non-pedagogical factors play major role in the teaching learning situation. Even if teacher wishes to teach his students language items or functional aspects, he is forced to follow the content oriented teaching due to above mentioned constraints. Classroom sizes are also responsible for ineffective teaching. Another important reason is uneven standard of students.

Some enterprising teachers, very few in number, experiment with non-conventional methods including use of audio-visual aids. But there is no uniform policy and provision for the use of these teaching equipments even to colleges where they are available for use. The reasons are lack of interest and aggravated by the chronic power problem. There is no uniform and consistent standard in the use of these teaching aids which is obvious from teachers' response. Teachers do not have only distinct individual styles of teaching, they also pursue different objectives in teaching the language and their approaches to the language are also different (*see* Chapter 4).

All teaching institutions are not of the same category. They have varied range of students who on the basis of their educational and family background, come from widely different socio-economic milieu. Premier colleges, where admission is restricted and is on the basis of marks scored at the school final stage, the response was quite encouraging, but those colleges where admission is liberal, the performance is very poor. Most of the students admitted in these colleges belong to rural areas and adjoining tarrai region of Nepal. Most of the teachers in these colleges are local young persons who join the job as part-time occupation in these colleges which do not pay regular salaries to these teachers, appointed on *ad hoc* basis. Any attempt at improving the teaching environment in these colleges is apt to prove futile in such a situation. The attitude of such teachers is either very casual or purely commercial. They have hardly any opportunity to join the refresher or orientation courses offered by the UGC for the improvement of teaching in colleges.

It is in this context of complex situation that the present study is expected to acquaint the experts with the "special condition" and problems of ELT in the area under study.

One of the reasons for the prevailing anarchy in the ELT situation is the total collapse of the examination system. English teaching and learning, it is felt, have become meaningless because the crucial ritual of examination is reduced to a farce. Examinations, however faulty they are in terms of evaluating the proficiency level of a learner, still encourage intensive teaching/learning activities. The "falling apart" of the system has created a situation in which "the best lacks all convictions" whereas irresponsible persons masquerading as educators are exploiting the situation.

These above mentioned variables are part and parcel of language teaching. Negligence of any of these causes imbalance in the whole teaching/learning situations. All these variables are discussed in later chapters to present a micro-level insight into the problem. The following questions which are very often raised by a number of teachers and parents are:

1. Does teaching of English make students know how to use the language for their future needs?
2. Do they understand what they are told outside the classroom?
3. Whether they can read any piece of information of their own and interpret it?
4. Whether they can do their written work successfully in any given circumstance?

To answer these questions, present study try to search out

problematic areas in teaching/learning situation and suggest appropriate remedial measures. To overcome these factors this study attempts to understand the part played by different variables in the teaching/learning process of forms and functions of English in the multilingual setting of Darbhanga.

Theoretical and Methodological Framework and its Goal

The research methods in this study involve both primary and secondary sources of data exemplifying the forms and functions of English in Darbhanga. For primary sources, I have relied exclusively on written texts. In that sense, this method may be called textual because the generalisations have been made on the basis of written texts and dissertation and not on the basis of first-hand observation of verbal interaction. I have used English language newspapers, magazines, journals and college textbooks.

I have not used phonological data from primary sources due to the tremendous variations in English pronunciation resulting from the other languages used in the place. A considerable body of phonological data is available in the primary sources which I have consulted, namely the previously discussed published research on the forms and functions of English.

I have made statistical correlation between linguistic forms and contexts of language use. I have analysed the data on the basis of secondary sources (data collected from questionnaire and personal interviews) have reinterpreted the data from the primary sources (texts and dissertations) with a view to supporting the following claims:

It hypothesises that:

1. Poor learning are manifestations of different constraints faced by learners.
2. Socio-cultural context and situation provide the ground for the type of learning takes place.
3. Degrees and types of nativisation of English vary directly with relative range and depth of English language and other languages in the linguistic repertoires of speech fellowships using English.

4. Any change in different variables affect the degree and type of teaching/learning situation.

The goal of this study is not only to describe in minute details of different constraints but also to demonstrate that:

1. A new perspective is needed for describing and interpreting use of non-native English, and
2. That this perspective can have important implications for linguistic theory and its applications.

2

Conventional English Teaching Methodology

Premisses and Practices

Introduction

There is a wide gap in terms of performance in the use of English between an average learner of this area and that of one, who follows almost the same course in a school outside the state. Julian Edge (1990) has given an interesting analogy to describe the ELT situation. This analogy is relevant in presenting the ELT situation in Darbhanga. He says:

> "Imagine a planet where the richest and most powerful countries develop a tradition of teaching classes of a hundred students. The best educational minds of each generation apply themselves to perfecting the best language teaching methods. One year, another planet is discovered; a poor, sparsely populated planet where life is hard and learners meet only in groups of ten. Imagine the problems of applying good methods in these impoverished circumstances. How can one adopt the ideal groups of ten communing technique to a context where one has only ten individuals to work with. Everyday, teachers all over this poor planet trudge to work with this and similar problems to contend with".

This is an unfair analogy and has some exaggerations also. But why should we believe that the way in the application and adaptation of other solutions is quite suitable for our students. Of course, we can learn from other people, but we can best act out an understanding of our own situation. There are many different situations all over India. The standards used in metropolitan cities and areas are quite different from those followed in semi-urban and rural areas. The difference lies not in the objectives but in the teaching-learning situations.

Conventional English Teaching and its Variables

For an in-depth study of English teaching situation in the area selected, we shall have to make a scientific study of the various aspects involved in teaching/learning process of English language. Since the issues are not only closely interlinked but also overlapping, a certain amount of repetition is unavoidable. In order to avoid repetitions readers are referred to proceeding and succeeding references in the chapter. The main aspects involving are as follows:

1. Teachers
2. Students
3. Evaluation and testing
4. Policy making for education and syllabus
5. Materials and teaching aids
6. Methodology
7. Socio-cultural variable
8. Guardian, society and non-linguistic factors.

Teachers

"Education is the manifestation of the perfection already in man", says Swami Vivekanand. It is like a lamp in a cask of iron. The teacher gradually unveils it. Therefore, the teacher has an important position in our tradition. If new teaching aids and machines are supplied to the learners for learning, relieving a teacher from his age old jobs, the elaborate Jaggernaut may not still be moved unless the whole system is set in motion on a set course, pushed, pulled and steered by teachers.

Today ELT situation is quite different from what it was a few years back. Today learners are more exposed to English through cinema, VCP and TV. A couple of decades ago there was no English movies but now English movies are regularly screened and video cassettes are available in remote villages. TV advertisements also play a vital role through its rhymes and zingles. But the paradox is that the learners were not benefited by these 'uncontrolled' exposures. These factors have developed an urge which is not properly channelised. The changing status of English has changed the age old role of the teacher. Now they have a number of different roles to perform. Their learners are not virgin stuff since they are already introduced to the language before they join schools. Therefore, the teacher has to monitor and co-ordinate their needs and skills. He has to act as a facilitator. He has to motivate them. The crucial role of the teacher is as a manager using teaching materials and technical media. It is a fact that no other technical equipment can take his place in the classroom.

Realising the importance of teacher in our teaching/learning process, we try to find out the factors which have a profound bearing on the teaching/learning process. There was a rich tradition of teacher-student relationship in India. But with the change in social dynamics and value scales, the old is yielding place to the new. In an article in *Hindustan* (dated 2-9-1990:6) a vivid picture of teachers working in the present situation comes before us. The economic and social pressure affects the standard of teaching. Most of them, in Bihar, are not properly and regularly paid. Their pay and perks are not in keeping with their tasks and responsibility. Their social position and prospect are not *at par* with other professionals. They have hardly any job satisfaction due to the prevailing anarchy caused by political interference and lack of financial support. Teaching environments are no less polluted than our environment. One of the big problems is of spurious texts and *bazar* notes which, by the forces of market manipulation, have driven out standard texts from book-stalls.

The change in social values also effects the moral of teachers. If some teacher wants to do his work faithfully he does not get encouragement from the institution due to personal prejudices. A number of students negate any attempt at improvement of teaching standard. It is beyond a teacher's capacity to handle a crowd of students hailing from different social, economic and cultural background. There is a total lack of personal contact with students.

The career of a teacher, in many cases, has become the last refuse of a brilliant (at least academically) but frustrated young man. They have no zeal left in them. They have neither training nor orientation.

They do not have any active role in syllabus design and question setting. Therefore, most of them are ignorant of the objectives of the course and do not know, if asked, why a particular book or a piece is being taught by him. They do not have either the direction or the training to motivate their students. Most of them follow the age old lecture method which makes the learners passive and listless.

Time factor is another problem. There are 3 or 4 classes (of 45-50 minutes, duration) per week. Insufficiency of time causes rapid teaching to finish the syllabus and the emphasis shifts from imparting language proficiency to completing the syllabus somehow.

The other problematic area in foreign language teaching is how to engage students' attention on text, both in their written and spoken forms. Developing learners' habit to look closely at text can often be seen as a major task that confronts every language teacher.

Our students opt for English to acquire interactional skills and language proficiency. They wish to speak clearly, accurately and intelligibly to share their experiences and exchange personal views and opinions. At this juncture the role of teacher is to instil confidence in the learner. If the learner had no confidence, then it would lead to a 'downward spiral' where both the teacher and the students might experience a sense of failure. The 'downward spiral' occurs when the teacher tries something new which leaves the student bemused, bewildered and insecure. The student then reacts badly. The teacher, consequently, becomes defensive and may try to force an activity on the students, who in turn, become hostile. As a result, both the teacher and the student fail to achieve their respective objectives. Therefore, the teacher has to dilute the lesson by extra linguistic components. Nolasco (1989) made certain interesting observations about the important role that body language played in teaching such as smile, forward lean, eye contact, nod, etc. A resourceful teacher can make his teaching interesting and does his task effectively not only by applying modern techniques but by adopting these non-linguistic devices also. All these make a performing teacher more effective and functional than any robot teacher, who takes over the job of teaching from teacher.

To accomplish a task successfully, it requires:

(a) involvement of students, and
(b) active participation and support of the teacher.

The teacher has to encourage the student by using such expressions like 'really', 'that's right', 'how interesting', 'exactly', etc. But unfortunately, the teachers here have hardly any time to make thus students involved in their teaching. Some other physical factors are listed as clarity, acoustics, distractions/noise, lapse in concentration, not knowing the subject, audibility, pace, intonation/ pronunciation, motivation, unfamiliar register, style, quality of voice. Our teachers are not aware of these physical components of effective teaching. Let us try to find out the functions assigned and performed by the teacher.

The pre-requisites for an effective teacher, says Palmer (1962) are his knowledge of the foreign language and of the student's native tongue, and ability to organise the programme, to choose the appropriate material and the most appropriate means of conveying and of inculcating it. That is to say, one who is prepared to conduct the pupil from his starting point, to his final goal treating all the aspects of language en route.

Other functions of the teacher are : to stimulate the pupil to work; to give the pupil opportunities of hearing the language spoken, and to act the part of second person in a conversation and to act as examiner, to award marks, and to correct errors. Besides organizing the programme and determining the manner in which the material is to be assimilated by the pupils, the teacher will take all the active measures necessary to stimulate the pupils in their task of assimilation. He must help them to digest the primary matter and must help them to produce the secondary matter. However well organised a programme of study may be, it will be inoperative if the stimulus is not present to act as the main spring of the perfect mechanism. At this point a teacher has to drive them. In every individual there are to be found latent capacities of intense interest and enthusiasm, in the case of children these capacities become active in strange ways. It is for the teacher to develop these latent capacities, to direct them into useful channels and to utilise them.

Actually, the teacher acts as an agent of change. Therefore, at the beginning of the year and throughout its course, the teacher must find out what all members of the class group have already learned in order to establish which behaviour to teach should have priority. Objectives can then be expressed to the pupils in such a way that they know at the outset what is expected of them and what are the important features of the task, rather than be told on presenting a carefully punctuated piece of work. Expressing objectives helps a teacher to plan the student's learning experiences, to pinpoint what each student needs to learn and to track their progress. This helps the teacher to see when students are not learning efficiently or quickly enough and to plan extra help when needed. If the teacher is to monitor student's work and evaluate progress, systematic record keeping procedures are vital. All these help the teacher in effective communication with the pupils.

To establish and maintain the role of a teacher depends upon the successful organisation and performance. He has been fully aware of the selection of the educational tasks. From a management point of view, curriculum planning and the choice of appropriate tasks are the essential starting points from which all other educational-setting events follow. Therefore, teachers need to try and find ways of presenting activities, particularly those which learners find less appealing, so as to overcome their initial inertia and increase their motivation. A teacher can add variety by working on the common sense, principle that a change is as good as a rest. During planning and preparing learner's work, a teacher, who is concerned with variety, not only considers what students are to learn from their tasks and which tasks are appropriate to their present skills and needs. He has to use the dimensions on which tasks can be varied so as to incorporate interest value and sustain students involvement.

The final aspect of the teacher's performance concerns sensitivity in the group and to the individuals within it. Responsiveness involves taking an active interest in the student and what they are doing. It also involves a willingness to act upon learner's reactions and to be flexible with them.

The essential ingredients of consequences, which a teacher uses to strengthen behaviour, are feedback and reinforcement. Students are not always aware of the behaviour they show, nor do they always notice the consequences of their behaviour in response to particular circumstances. Occasionally when learning new behaviour, it may be noticed that they obtained the outcome they desired, but without realising what they did was appropriate. So when a teacher provides feedback to students, he helps them overcome these difficulties by establishing these connections for them. He may point out that a behaviour was appropriate and may underline the links between a behaviour and its consequences. Feedback is, therefore, crucial when teaching new skills.

Students

Next to the teachers, an attempt is made to analyse in some detail student's part played in the language learning procedure and language teaching situations. We find that a large number of so-called English medium schools have mushroomed all over the country, because English is believed to be the language of opportunity and all parents want their children to grow up speaking English. At the age of three when the young child goes to school, he is alienated from his mother tongue, and what he is given in its place is a great deal of bad English. At the end of his schooling, he does not know the proper use of either his mother tongue or English or any language for that matter. He ends up by having not only badly structured language, but also badly organised thinking and wrongly formed concepts.

At least in Darbhanga, the greatest problem regarding ESL teaching is the non-availability of secondary school teachers possessing any English worth speaking of. This being the case, we are promoting the propagation of deplorably un-English like forms of English by our insistence on the communicating use of the language in our secondary school classrooms. We insist upon practices which do more harm than good to our ESL learners. Therefore, the learning of some sound English is more preferable than the learning of a great deal of language that can hardly be called English; our learners never usually manage to unlearn all these and it is an alarming fact.

At this point there arise a number of important questions:

(a) Do all our learners need to learn to speak English?

(b) Granted that they do, are we justified in giving them totally unacceptable varieties of spoken English?

(c) If the secondary school curriculum has given them some sound conscious knowledge about basic rules and forms in English and if this is all that it can manage to give them, will not this knowledge stand them in good stead when later circumstances expose them to communicative use of English? At least will they not have the ability to discriminate behaviour acceptable and unacceptable and unacceptable forms, and perhaps to decide to imitate the acceptable forms.

To meet these questions, an extensive field work was conducted by Das in 1989. This fieldwork includes cultural anthropology and social psychology, along with courses in ELT. H.G. Widdowson (1971) refers to the following components of a complete ELT programme as a second language:

(a) Learner's aim;
(b) Student's age, intelligence, educational and cultural background and motivation;
(c) The geographical situation, political affiliations and economic conditions of the place;
(d) Internal linguistic situation;
(e) Guardian and society;
(f) Teacher's training, experience and cultural background;
(g) Size of class and time allotted to class;
(h) Difference between L_1 and L_2;
(i) Course materials and teaching aids;
(j) Methodology; and
(k) Evaluation.

Palmer (1964) states that one cannot determine 'what is the best method adopting the best means towards the required end' until one knows more precisely what is the required end. For there are many possible ends, and many categories of students, each with a particular aim before him. A course, which is suitable in one case, may prove unsuitable in another. Some students may require only knowledge of the written language, others desire to become conversant with both aspects. Some require a superficial knowledge, while others aim at a perfect knowledge, some want to specialise, others wish to become proficient as translators or interpreters or the sole aim of some students is to pass a given examination. It is the duty of teachers to cater to the students' need in order to obtain satisfactory results. Learners, having entirely different aims, require entirely different methods; they must be furnished with everything that will facilitate their work and omit from their programme everything which does not lead directly towards the special aim they have in view. For communicative use of language, Rama (1989) observes, the learners' basic aim in learning English are to:

— Speak clearly, accurately and intelligibly;
— Communicate effectively;
— Maintain and develop simple conversations;
— Share experiences;
— Exchange personal views and opinions;
— Tell an anecdote;
— Word with others; and
— Give a short talk.

The function of conversation was identified as exchange of information, developing and sustaining social relationship, negotiation of social status and roles, deciding on and carrying out joint actions. The syllabus would, therefore, have to include, interrelate and integrate the following: Language proficiency, interactional skills, cultural background. But due to large number of students in a class, teacher's lack of awareness towards the learner's aim, time factor available, non-flexible course-content imposed by the university are obstacles to the attainment of the objectives. It is impossible for a teacher to cope with the diversified aim of the students in a very little time. If they identify learners' aim then they have no freedom to choose appropriate material for the desired end. The prescribed course content have variegated materials, no doubt, but every aspect of language cannot be taught within a fixed period of time to approximately 50 or sometimes more than 100 students according to their aims. It will take more time and hard work. In fact, most of our teachers are not aware of the fact that learners' aim takes an important role in teaching English.

Evidently, it will not be possible to draw up a programme of study which will be suitable for all the diversed requirements. Nor will it be possible for every teacher to consider the individual requirements of each one of his pupils. We cannot have a specially printed course for every student. It can be possible only in case of private lessons or of self-instruction courses.

Students' age, intelligence, educational and cultural background also play a major role in learning L_2. The young child engaged at an early age in the development of his faculties of speech is doing so with perfect unconsciousness and without any regard to the principle of segregation (Palmer 1968). The adult student, grappling with problems of the etymological order, concentrates the whole of his attention to that which is the immediate object of his study, and thus follow rule of segregation.

V.J. Cook (1982) finds that an important factor in second language learning is the learner's age. Some Canadian research showed that children under the age of 7 fared better at learning English than those who arrived at an older age (Ramsay and Wright, 1974). There is a mass of evidence that adults are either superior to or the same as children. Adults are better than children at understanding spoken Russian by the total physical response method (Asher and Price, 1967); teenagers are better at learning grammar than younger children in English (Fathaman, 1975). (V.J. Cook, 1982). Nine-year olds learn French morphology and syntax faster than four year olds (Ervin-Tripp 1974). But the most general is that there is a critical period for language learning; after we have left the period we can learn language only with difficulty. The reasons for this may be lateralisation; *i.e.*, the tendency for brain functions to become specialised to one side or the other in the early teens (Scovel, 1969). Krashen claims that the distinctive feature of adult 'learning' is that adults can monitor what they are producing but advanced learners have not been found to be better at correcting their own mistakes than the beginners.

Due to fully developed reasoning power, an adult learner's difficulties often turn into perplexity, bewilderment or confusion of thought, a state of mind which precludes any possibility of effective progress. Teachers are unable to do anything positive towards removing the mental block. Actually, the degree of success attained by adults in their efforts to acquire a foreign language is always in direct ratio to the degree in which they observe the natural laws of language study. Most persons taking up their residence abroad acquire with remarkably rapidity and fidelity the speech of those by whom they are surrounded, provided that they observe certain conditions. These conditions are generally assumed to consist of the exercising of their powers of observations and imitation, unaided by such artificial processes as translation, etymological analysis and synthesis or the mental conversion of written into spoken forms.

In support of this theory, it has been pointed out that the illiterate often seems to succeed due to his ignorance and unformed mental capacities, where the scholar will be handicapped by his developed intellect. In fact, the active use of speech under natural condition is invariably preceded by a period during which a certain proficiency is attained in its passive aspect. Actually all these factors are responsible for their insufficient learning and our adult students often feel bewildered and confused. They never get enough opportunities of cognising the language passively. It is an undoubted fact that the active use of speech under natural conditions is invariably preceded by a period during which a certain proficiency is attained in its passive aspect. The faculty of recognizing and of understanding the units of speech is probably always developed by the child long before he ever reproduces them in order to make himself understood.

On the basis of intelligence we can classify students into the following categories:

(a) bad pupil,
(b) bad learner, and
(c) slow learner.

By bad pupil we mean, the one who will not work. The lazy fellow, we can only advise him. The slow learner is one who has no natural gift for language. He is, by no means, a hopeless case. If he is docile and does what a competent teacher tells him to do and works conscientiously he is not a bad learner, merely a slow one. But by bad learner we mean the intelligent type of student who either from want of reflection or from ignorance of language and its nature, misdirects all his efforts, does what he ought not to do and leaves undone all that he ought to do. Bad learners are characterised by:

(a) thoughtlessness or lack of reflection – has conception of the nature of language or its study;
(b) mistaken haste – in such a hurry to work that he forgets to buy tools;
(c) prejudice – over confidence in some particular system and too little confidence in others;
(d) lack of proportionate discernment – exaggerates or else he unduly belittles difficulties or forms a mistaken analogy between language learning and other subjects of study; and
(e) 'old fogeyism' – the incapacity to absorb new ideas combined with an instinctive fear of the unknown.

There are many types of bad learners, and the mixed and

bewildering nature of their vagaries renders these so complex as to defy classification (for details please see Palmer, 1968).

Confronted with a new language the learner applies certain strategies with conscious and unconscious to what he hears, which partly determine his language system (Selinker, 1972; Richards, 1971). The positive effects of the learner's conscious awareness that he is learning a new language have been described in terms of the strategies that the learner adopts. Though these strategies necessarily appear 'obvious', any model of second language learning to take them into account; if, for instance, adult learners feel that L_2 learning is chiefly a matter of vocabulary (Hatch, 1976). This clearly has an effect on their learning, regardless of whether they are right or wrong. The learner then, consciously or unconsciously, absorbs or extracts information from what he hears. Selinker suggests the strategy to impose the structure of his L_1: he transfers rules or items to his (learner)—language system from his L_1 and shows signs of 'interference' (1972). Taylor's proposed strategy is to attempt to guess the system of the target language, resulting in 'overgeneralisation', his use of this strategy increases as he learns more of language, (1975). The learner also pays great attention to word order (Chun 1976; Lattey, 1975). He may appear to 'simplify' the L_2: his sentences have a similar grammar and use reduced forms, similar in many ways to a pidgin language. In general, the conscious and unconscious strategies that the learner employs are of vital importance and we need to know more about them, not only in linguistic terms but also in the cognitive and social terms (Chun, 1975; Filmore, 1976).

In present context, it is found that in L_2 class, the tasks attempted by the learners are so far out of the reach of their linguistic capabilities that their struggle for performance results in the production of language which only very remotely resembles acceptable varieties of the language taught. It is clear that our learners mostly belong to the third group (slow).

Cook (1982) asserts that the way in which a learner learns a L_2 is also affected by his attitudes and psychological motivations. The two main types of motivations that have been described are the 'integrative' in which the learners want to communicate actively with the speaker of the other language, and the 'instrumental', in which he wants to use the language for some utilitarian purpose. Success in L_2 learning depends on the attitude towards the foreign culture, towards learning a foreign language, and towards the classroom situation

(Gardner *et al.*, 1976). One's native language is an important factor in one's sense of identity as an individual and as a member of a group: learning a new language means adopting a new identity.

The internal linguistic situation of the place also effects student's performance. Darbhanga has a predominance of Maithili speakers. Most of the students have Maithili as their L_1 or MT. This language is spoken in the Northern region of Bihar. Though it is spoken all over Bihar, its maximum occurrence is seen in and around Darbhanga. It was once considered to be a dialectal variation of Hindi. Maithili speakers' attitude to learn English is not different from the speakers of other languages. They consider it a prestigious language and there is a strong feeling that acquisition of this language ensures social prestige and even professional competence.

The essential format in class exercise, no matter how beneficial, provides very little experience in coping with the interactive use of spoken English as it is found in the wider community outside the EL classroom. Students feel that they have difficulty in English conversation, and avoid speaking English outside the classroom. They confuse the English idioms with native expressions and accents which are altogether different from Indian languages.

The geographical and economic conditions of the place have their impact on learning/teaching situation. Among the students studying here, about 59.2 per cent opt for English. 77.9 per cent of them belong to science stream and they opt for English for higher studies, and among the arts students 3.01 per cent offer this subject. There is almost nil interaction with native speakers of English. For day-to-day works people use either Maithili or Hindi, hence they are exposed to English only in the classroom situation.

The other factors, such as guardians and society, teacher, class size, course content, difference between L_1 and L_2 and evaluation system, also influence students' performance. These components are discussed in different sections of this chapter.

Policy Making Design for Education and Syllabus

In recent years, increasing attention has been paid to the learning and teaching of English. The reasons, according to Trim (1978), for this change has been manifold. It may be simply a question of exposure to information and entertainment media, books, newspapers, films, radio and television or may be for any occupational need. It is self evident that English has assumed great importance as an international medium of communication and has created a demand for the language on a vast scale. To meet the demands of diverse, complex and rapidly changing situations, more conscious appraisal of national policy on language, needs and demands is called for, so that a sensible language policy can be devised. Language planning of this sort has to cover both internal and external language relations. It is in the light of this appraisal that the allocation of resources for the encouragement and organisation of language learning has to be made.

The face-validity of these types of language teaching, says Strevens (1978), rests upon the specification of the learners' particular purpose, a process which delimits and restricts the learners' agenda, and by implication makes all the learning relevant and therefore secures good motivation and by popular repute leads to relatively high rates of achievement and of learner-satisfaction.

The entire situation has been analysed in depth in the Report of the Curriculum Development Centre in English, CIEFL, Hyderabad as a UGC Project (1989). It has been felt in academic circles that schools and universities in India had not kept pace with the fast changing needs and demands of the society. Such feeling has been clearly expressed in the *Programme of Action* (1986) on the national policy on education. "The courses offered by the universities have not been recognised to meet the demands of the times. Their relevance and utility are constantly questioned. The credibility of the evaluation system is being eroded".

Our students come from widely divergent home, school and social backgrounds and cannot therefore be expected to have even roughly comparable levels of proficiency in English (This fact has been truer because of the official policies of some boards of education, under which a student is declared successful even if he has failed in English). And yet, no university makes provision for students with widely different linguistic attainments in English to choose, at the undergraduate level, courses in English appropriate for their linguistic level. Far from this, a typical college curriculum in English does not attempt to address itself to the average student.

As for the linguistic demands of future employment, many of the newer jobs, which have become available relatively recently, demand a fair degree of proficiency in the use of the present day English, both spoken as well as written. Here again, our university courses have not tried to meet this demand.

The blame may be put on poor teaching at the school level. Other factors generally held responsible are large size of classes, indifferent students and teachers, inappropriate teaching materials, inefficient methods, testing techniques that fail to test proficiency in the language and so on. But one important factor that is sometimes overlooked is that in some states the official policy on the teaching of English has not remained stable. No other single factor can affect the status of English in the curriculum more seriously than such a situation. No teacher or student will pay more attention to a subject of learning than is demanded by the official status accorded to it in the curriculum. And the status accorded to English by many boards of education and universities has suffered a serious setback. Whereas before Independence, English was a compulsory subject in both school and college courses, it did not remain so in several parts of the country after Independence. What is even worse is that there are universities that do prescribe English as a compulsory subject at the under-graduate level, but do not do full justice to it. In some universities, though it is taught as a compulsory subject, it does not carry any credit : it does not count towards a student's success or otherwise in an examination and/or his overall grade/division/class. What is more, very few universities allot it more than two or three periods a week (thus treating it as a half subject), not realizing that learning of a language involves the development of certain skills in it, and this necessitates the allotment of more time, not less than allotted to any other subject of study.

Decisions regarding the criteria of teaching any subject (English) and its position and status in the teaching schedule of students are made by the 'Inter University Board'. It is an autonomous body which gives direction to all universities of Bihar regarding the criteria for syllabus. But universities have no freedom to select teaching materials and frame out the courses according to their needs. Academic Council and Board of Studies of university concerned introduce teaching materials within the framework of courses and syllabi prescribed by the Bihar Inter University Board. Janice Yalden (1983) points out that the primary preoccupation of the syllabus designer must be to decide what components will be included in a given syllabus and in what proportion or with what emphasis. Decisions of this sort are generally made on the basis of the following:

(a) As acquiring a body of linguistic knowledge;
(b) As acquiring a new set of habits or changing linguistic behaviour; and
(c) As being able to interact in a social situation in an effective way.

In an approach to designing a model, as John Munby (1978) puts it, the problem was considered in terms of a set of hierarchically ordered parameter maps, the first layer being an abstract or general representation of what were taken to be the salient features, the second showing the constitutions of the parameters, given a specific type of learner.

In Fig. 2.1, variables, of the kind influenced by adoption of a particular theoretical perspective, operate as constraints on a language learner to identify his goals. Three potential dimensions of syllabus specification, seen as behaviour domain determinants, formal determinants and situational determinants, will then reflect the goals.

In Fig 2.2, a specific category of second language participant has specific communicative objectives, which are achieved by controlling particular communicative behaviour. There was then a third layer where all the appropriate realisations take place.

Janice Yaldin (1983), says that before designing a course, the course designer should enable to achieve two things:

(a) Produce a detailed profile of what the learner needs to be able to do in English in the occupation or studies for which he is being trained, and
(b) Produce a specification of the language skills, functions and forms required to carry out the communication described in the needs profile.

As a consequence of the requirement, that a designer should analyse the needs of a learner, these needs are increasingly stated in communicative terms: in terms of what it is that learner opting for his future jobs, normally he wants to do through language. It is stated in

Theoretical Framework

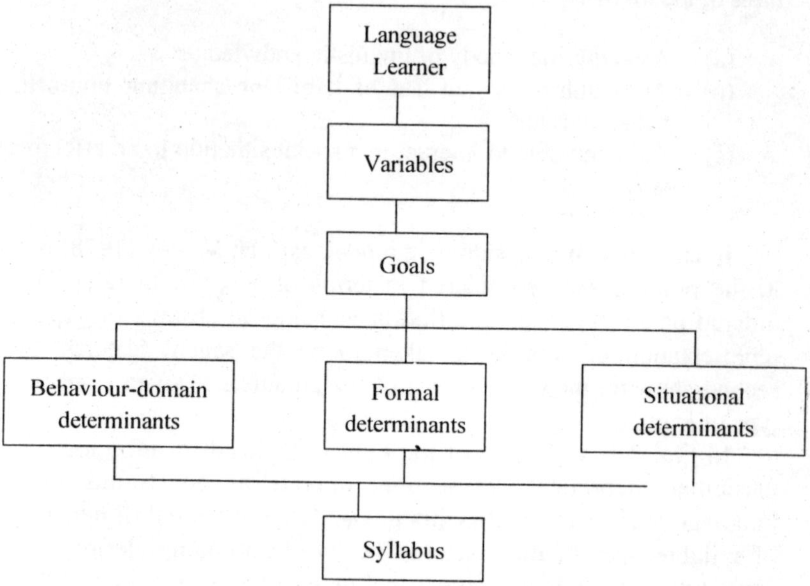

Fig. 2.1: Parameter Map: Layer 1 (General)

terms of communicative categories to which would be appended illustrations of the actual spoken and written language which will be taught. These categories could be, according to Peter Strevens (1978):

(a) General Communication,
(b) Social Communication, and
(c) Special Communicative Purpose.

An analysis of these prescribed courses makes it obvious that learner's language requirements are either to meet their educational needs or occupational needs.

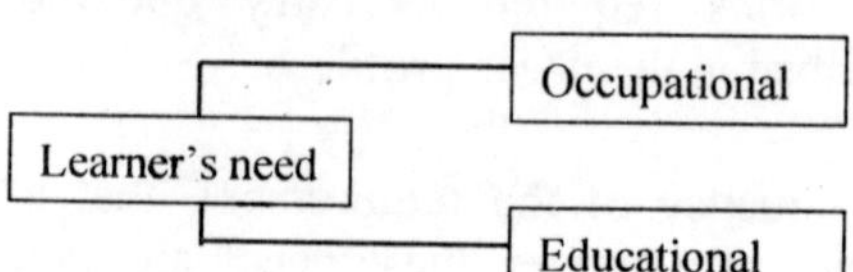

Theoretical Framework

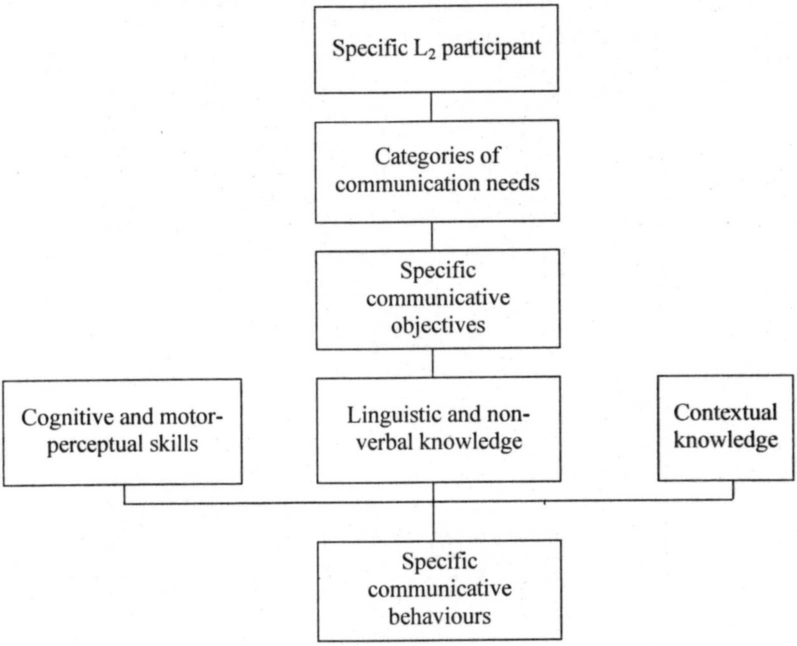

Fig. 2.2: Parameter Map: Layer 2 (Specific)

This distinction becomes important in practice, since job-oriented learners are usually more pragmatic, intolerant of what they feel to be irrelevant. Critical of unauthentic materials, keen to achieve effective communication but contemptuous of aesthetic niceties such as elegance of style, native like pronunciation etc. In addition, students of occupational need tend to be less academic to have less previous language learning experience to have fixed ideas (often in conflict with their teachers) about how they should be taught, and to be self conscious about returning to the classroom a settled career. They usually welcome role playing or role simulation techniques (Currie, Sturtridge & Allwright, 1972).

Both educational and occupational language teaching courses require to be subdivided according to whether the language training precedes, follows or is simultaneous with their studies or occupational training.

Since English is opted for these reasons, Peter Strevens (1978) reiterates that the courses should take these considerations in mind. So these distinctions are presented in Fig. 2.3.

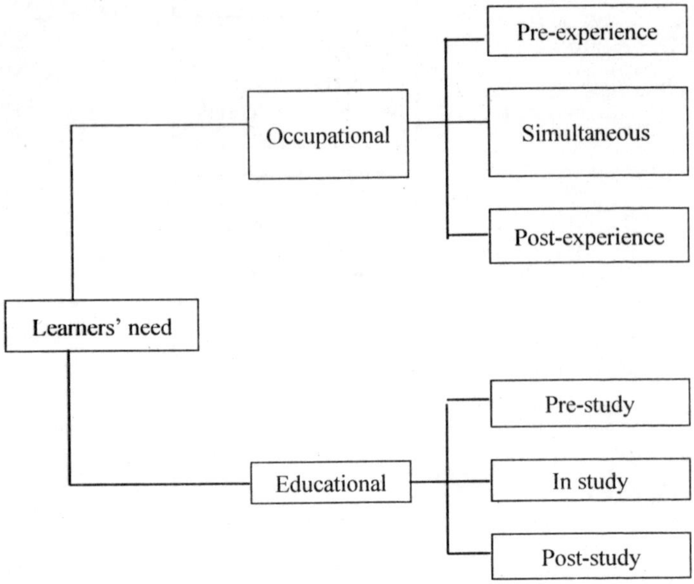

Fig. 2.3: Important Considerations

Quite apart from the scientific/non-scientific dimension referred to earlier, it is essential, in practice, to distinguish different frameworks of education (school, university, adult education etc.) to allow for differences of quantity, intensity and duration of instruction and to make appropriate changes according to the starting level of learner's proficiency (beginner, false beginner, intermediate, advanced). A detailed discussion on these variables has been presented by Strevens (1977c).

In the Communication Needs Processor (John Munby, 1978), it is preferable to take account of the variables that affect communication needs by organising them as parameters in a dynamic relationship to each other. These parameters are of two kinds: those that process non-linguistic data and those that provide the data in the first place, *i.e.*, one set of constraints (*a posteriori*) that depend upon impute from another set of constraints (*a priori*) before they can become operational. The *priori* parameters are:

(a) Purposive domain
(b) Setting
(c) Interaction
(d) Instrumentality

The *posteriori* parameters are:

(a) Dialect
(b) Target level
(c) Communicative event
(d) Communicative key

The dependency relationships (what is affected by what) result from the processing in each of the eight parameters as the profile of communication needs for that particular participant or category of participants.

It is noticeable that the profile is a detailed description of particular communication needs without containing any specification of the actual language forms that will realise those needs. Therefore, it operates at the pre-language stage in the specification of communicative competence. But misunderstanding the nature of communication needs also show itself when matters of logistics or pedagogy are included as variables in the consideration of the participants' communication needs. For example, the number of teachers available, the intensity or length of the course, financial considerations, the learner's attitude towards teachers and his previous learning methods are all important factors for consideration in the organisation of the programmes and the construction of the materials, but they are irrelevant to the specification of what the learner needs – the target language, which comprises his communi-cation needs.

Language Skills Selector

In this parameter of the overall model, the profile of needs is interpreted in terms of the specific language skills that are required to realise the events or activities that have been identified as the communication need processor (CNP). Syllabus designers as well as writers of books on the teaching of English as a second language regularly divide up their subject into oral comprehension, oral production, reading comprehension and written production. In selecting the skills, recourse is taken both to introspection and to any relevant stylistic information available.

In the case of some occupational type activities, it may be found that socio-semantic processing will be more fruitful than skill selection, the essential instrumentality features such as the medium and mode in which the functional sub-categories are to be handled having already been specified in the CNP.

The Meaning Processor

In this component of the model, parts of the socio-culturally determined profile of communication needs are converted into semantic sub-categories of a predominantly pragmatic kind and marked for attitudinal tone. Here the consideration must be of the kind of semantic unit that needs to be handled and the nature of the conversion and the argument for such processing in the first place.

Candlin (1976) suggests that there are four possible levels or layers of meaning for an utterance, which are described as notional, referential, socio-linguistic and contextual meaning.

Converting events into their meaning units at the first layer, *i.e.*, into conceptual categories, is unlikely to be significant for subsequent encoding. For Leech and Svartvic (1975), the first layer of meaning includes concepts such as cause, purpose, condition and comparison. The types of meaning handled by Leech and Svartvic (1975) at their second layer (information, reality and belief) as categories of logical communication. The third layer of meaning concerns with mode, emotion and attitude. The fourth layer of meaning consists of the utterance's contextual meaning. That is, part of its meaning derives from what it precedes and what it follows.

The characterisation of communicative events as meaning sub-categories considered from the standpoint of pragmatics can therefore be described as esśentially socio-semantic processing. The term function is used in both a macro and micro sense. Candlin (1976) uses the term in both senses when he says, "Thus we can say that the utterance "I' ll fix you" can be seen to realise an act termed threat and threatening is associated with the function of language we have called social control. Here threatening is a micro function and social control a macro function. These micro functions, therefore, are units of meaning operating as an inter-level between events and their formal realisations. What has been considered then for is the kind of semantic unit that needs to be handled and how an activity is converted into such units. The direct encoding of a communicative event as lexico grammatical realisation is not a feasible proposition. It seems necessary first to do an analysis of the event into its activities where the communicative value can then be specified. Then it might be argued that one should go direct from the specification of the activities to the selection of forms for encoding or realising each activity, without socio-semantic processing. The functional analysis of communicative activities ensures that the socio-semantic aspect of communicative competence is given systematic and due attention in the learning of linguistic (and extra linguistic) forms.

Socio-semantic processing, then, characterises events in terms of micro functions which are marked for attitudinal tone.

Linguistic Encoding

In discussing the communicative competence the crucial importance was established of the dimension of contextual appropriacy in both the socio-cultural and discoursal senses of context, which is reflected in the constituents of the theoretical framework. The model being designed takes clear account of this in the profiling of communication needs and the subsequent sociosemantic processing. Now the linguistic encoding should be done, where the selection of the actual verbal relisations for the micro-functions and subject matter is made, and one has to face the problem of the criterion for our decisions as to appropriacy. That is, does one decide on matters of language variation in a particular context of use on the basis of introspection and one's own subjective judgement as a native speaker as to what is stereotypical, or is there an objective yardstick such as a 'dictionary of use' to which one can turn. This means, then, that we should take account of the gradually increasing amount of stylistic information on what forms of utterances are appropriate in a particular social context and how they cohere rhetorically in a particular discourse context. Recourse is taken then to any available stylistic information on distinctive features, rules of use, co-occurrence and distributional characteristics, which relate directly or indirectly, wholly or partly, to the microfunctions and language skills under consideration. If there is, it is used; if there is no relevant information in the 'bank', then one proceeds on a subjective basis and decides on the appropriate realisation(s) from a combination of one's own intuition, the intuition of suitable informants, and where necessary, a standard reference grammar and dictionary. It should be noted that such subjective decisions can always be empirically validated.

A General Framework of L_2 Education

Because of the complexity of the language situation and wide variety of needs, it is increasingly apparent that model curriculum for second language education should be general in nature and it will be adaptable to a wide variety of needs, but which, at the same time, will be based on a consistent methodology and underlying view of the language.

The traditional syllabus was essentially based on the same model. The selection and sequencing of linguistic structures only, the underlying assumption being that learning a language meant learning to master its grammatical system. In addition, it was expected that students would acquire a reasonably adequate basic vocabulary of a standard sort, no matter which method was employed (Janice Yalden: 1983).

In speaking of rules of use in applied linguistics, what has been missing from our language programmes is a consideration of how we use language in everyday situation, of all sorts. When we speak our own language, or any other that we know well, we concern ourselves with much more than linguistic accuracy as we go about a business. We express ourselves in an appropriate fashion as we move from one context to another and even as we function within any one context or situation. It is this quality of appropriateness that has been neglected in our teaching.

Courses are planned in such a way that the language items to be taught are ordered into a list of grammatical structure and a list of lexical items. The learner is exposed to a limited sample of the target language and the sample is carefully controlled by the teaching situation. The learner's job is thus to resynthesize language that has been taken apart and presented to him in small pieces. The teacher is concerned much more with knowledge of the language system than with its use. What happens in the classroom is that the teacher, in following the syllabus, may use either a grammar-translation method or an audio-lingual one or a combination of the two. Whichever he uses, the constraints are the same: the context of the syllabus has been determined by giving up top priority to teaching the 'grammar' or 'structure' of the language.

At the same time there was the advent of a desire to provide more 'ordinary' and less literary models of language. Steiner's (1970) discussion of performance objectives clarifies this point as follows:

> "If we state that one of our course objectives is to enable a student to communicate with others, no one will know what we actually mean in terms of particulars............. communicate how? In writing? With gesture? in speech? Fluency? Somewhat? In actually what we have considered an objective is a purpose .... our purposes are not served by using general verbs such as "understand, have an appreciation for, have a feeling for, know, enjoy believe".

What we need in foreign language teaching is to use specific verbs such as "to write in that language", to answer orally in that language, "to translate into written language, to read aloud, to select the correct answer for, ... And so on. He goes on to discuss the desirability of detailed specification and makes the distinction between purpose and objectives as follows:

A purpose states why a subject is being studied:

(a) to apply grammar correctly;
(b) to gain appreciation of literature; and
(c) to be able to communicate in.

An objective states specially what a student should be able to do under what circumstances and these objectives should lead him to his purpose.

The preparation of performance objectives represent a large step towards precision in defining the goals of a course of instruction.

Yalden (1983) puts his views after observing that "communication is unsystematic and predictable, but we use systematically learned and organised language to achieve it". He proposes 'proportional' curriculum which is similar to the 'variable focus' model developed at the Ontario Institute for Studies in Education. In this curriculum the aim of the model is to provide a coherent way of thinking about teaching which encourages the use of the widest possible range of classroom activities depending on the course objectives, the students' interests and abilities and the teacher's need. We begin by distinguishing between curriculum (a very general concept), syllabus (a sub-part of curriculum which is concerned with the itemisation of lesson content) and classroom methodology. Methodology in turn has two aspects:

(a) Material design, and
(b) Classroom processes.

The basic unit of organisation, according to Allen (1987), is that of the communicative setting which may be expressed in terms of topic, theme, or task. Once we have established the communicative setting for a lesson unit, it is necessary to consider the specific learning objectives in terms of a set of specifications drawn from two related syllabuses. The linguistic syllabus include details of grammatical categories, communicative functions and rules of discourse that will be taught over a period of time. Parallel to this is the non-linguistic syllabus which includes details of the conceptual content, knowledge of the world, etc., which will be required for carrying out a task, a productive analysis of one or more ways of performing the task, and conceptualisation of the principles of problem solving which will be involved.

As shown in Fig. 2.4, the linguistic syllabus and the non-linguistic syllabus are resources which are fed into classroom methodology, which contains three interrelated activity components: Type A — Grammatical practice, Type B — Guided discourse practice, and Type C — Experiential practice. Allen (1987) has dealt with the issue in great detail.

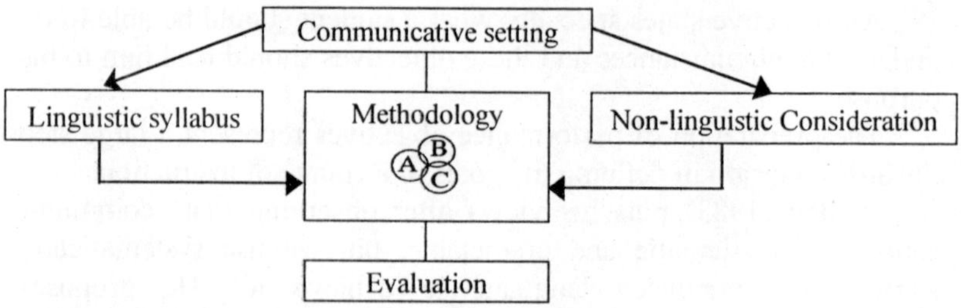

A: Grammatical practice; B: Guided discourse practice; C: Experiential practice.

Fig 2.4: A General Curriculum Framework for L_2 Education

In the foregoing paragraphs is given an overall view of the existing curriculum and what are the basics of a communicative curriculum. From this, we now proceed to a detailed account of the curriculum at the school and the undergraduate levels. The account is based on analysis of the existing syllabus which is prescribed by Bihar Secondary Examination Board, Inter University Board and Lalit Narayan Mithila University, Darbhanga and includes an observation and survey work.

The account is presented separately under the following heads:

(a) Place of English
(b) Patterning of courses
(c) Nature of course content
(d) Methodology
(e) Testing
(f) The teacher
(g) Administrative factors

Place of English

In spite of the attempts made by state governments and the central government to make regional language the media of instruction at the school and college level; there is still a general demand for instruction through English on the part of parents and students. However, college entrants are not sufficiently equipped with the language competency to pursue their studies through the medium of English. As against this, where regional languages are the media of instruction, suitable textbooks and reference materials are not available in these languages for each subject. Therefore, both in schools and university, where English is the medium of instruction as well as where the regional language is used, students require a good grounding in English for academic purposes. English is not compulsory subject at matriculation and also it is not a compulsory subject at undergraduate level.

Patterning of Courses

There are two papers of 75 marks each, at secondary level. On the other hand, NCERT secondary courses offer three types of compulsory English courses (English A, English B, and Remedial

English) to suit the different entry level proficiency of the learners.

At intermediate level there are two papers of 100 marks each. It is not compulsory. It comes in the category of subjects in the language group, if opted by student. They can choose it either as a language and literature course (a compulsory subject) or as an optional subject. They have other options too.

At BA level general English is not compulsory. Students have only elective English which is of three types—

(a) Special or Honours course in English.;
(b) Subsidiary course English; and
(c) General (Pass course) English.

Special or Honours course

Those students who opt for English to continue for higher studies opt for English Honours courses. In three-year degree course they have to study eight papers of 100 marks each. They have to study two papers in first year, two papers in the second year and remaining four papers in the third year.

Subsidiary Courses

Those students who opt for honours course in other subjects but like to study English, they can opt for it as a subsidiary subject. Then they have to study two papers of two hundred marks. One paper in the first year and the second paper in the second year.

General (Pass) Course

Those students who do not pursue Honours course and want to study English, they may offer it as one of the three pass course subjects. They have to study three papers of three hundred marks, one paper in each of the three years.

Nature of Course Content

Course content included in courses comprises of literary items and prose pieces (for detail please see Chapter 2 in section material and teaching aids).

Methodology

Syllabus does not impart any hint for methodology, adopted to teach items prescribed (for detail please see Chapter 2 in section methodology).

Testing

Syllabus presents account for testing. In brief, it imparts instructions on the pattern of question to be asked and about distribution of marks. No elaborate directions are given for evaluation (for detail please see Chapter 2 in section Evaluation and testing).

The Teacher

Teacher is the main architect behind the teaching/ learning scene. But syllabus does not present much information about any variables of teaching-learning situation (for detail please see Chapter 2 in section Teachers).

Administrative Factors

Though syllabus formation is a purely academic process but administrative factors play an important role in prescribing a syllabus for a particular course. It is already discussed earlier in this section.

After a close study of syllabus, it becomes obvious that syllabus for general purpose English needs radical changes to fulfil the new demands posited by the students.

Materials and Teaching Aids

It is surprising, and rather unfortunate, that a course in spoken English, for its non-native speakers, is considered either elitist or unnecessary, and looked upon as something beyond the range of subjects normally within the purview of an ordinary English teacher, states Chaudhary (1992). Studies by Bansal (1969), Black *et al.*, (1965) and many others have described the difficulties in spoken communication experienced by non-native users of English due to the neglect of spoken English.

Since Indian writers are appearing in ever increasing numbers in text books at Indian schools and colleges, it may seem strange to treat their usage as anything less than the model. Grafting a model of language insensitive to socio-cultural realities may not be easy. So there arises a question about the extent to which we can afford to deviate from a standard acceptable norm, opines Janice Yalden (1983). The kind of approach to language course design is the one traditionally adopted in our educational institution. The manner of setting about the task of course planning has come to be regarded as deficient which is reflected in the academic debates over method. It was recognised recently that no matter which 'method' was selected, any syllabus, that was produced, was essentially based on the same model, the selection and sequencing of linguistic structures only the underlying assumption being that learning a language means learning to matter its grammatical system. In addition, it was expected that students would acquire a reasonably adequate 'basic' vocabulary of a standard sort, again no matter which method was employed.

The acknowledgement of this difficulty in the second language learning and teaching process coincides with profound changes in the development of linguistic theory. A new form of alliance is becoming clear. Widdowson describes it as follows:

> "There is an increasing recognition of the need to pay as much attention to the rules of use, the speaker's communicative competence, as to rule of grammar, his grammatical competence, and that an adequate linguistic description must account for both (Widdowson 1979a : 12)".

In speaking of rules of use (in applied linguistic), we mean that what has been missing from our language programme is a consideration of how we use language in everyday situations of all sorts. When we speak our own language or any other that we know well, we concern ourselves with much more than linguistic accuracy as we go about our business. We also make sure that we express ourselves in an appropriate fashion as we move from one context to another even as we function within any one context or situation.

For someone who is still a learner of the language in which the conversation is being conducted, however, it is not easy to know what exactly ought to be said under these circumstances. The appropriate words and phrases which every language reserves for these occasions have to be specially learnt, for they can hardly ever be arrived at by literally translating the corresponding phrases of one's own language; but these conversational lubricants seldom find a place in language courses. Abercrombie (1963). It is this quality of appropriateness that has been neglected in our teaching materials.

In planning courses, the language items to be taught are ordered into a list of grammatical structures and a list of lexical items. The learner is exposed at any one time only to a limited sample of the target language and the sample is carefully controlled by the teaching situation. The learner's job is to resynthesize language that has been taken apart and presented to him in small pieces. A planned curriculum reflects the needs of learners and making sure that each learner is working on appropriate skills and task within it which are fundamental prerequisites for effective teaching. But if a learner is presented with a task which is too difficult, he is likely to delay starting or soon stop working. Similarly, if the task is too easy, again they are in a position of having nothing to do. Hence from the management point of view, appropriate task designings are essential starting points from which all other educational setting events follow. There are some dimensions on which task vary:

(a) Time to be spent;
(b) Complexity of the task;
(c) Presentation and format;
(d) What children are to do during the task;
(e) Amount of pupil choice;
(f) Amount of teacher's involvement; and
(g) Pattern of interaction.

It is suggested by Rod Ellis (1982) that if the materials are based on a description of what the learner is to acquire and it does not matter whether the description is based on a theory of linguistics of communicative competence — and are designed to focus on specific items of usage or use, then the condition under which acquisition can take place will not have been met for the environment will be 'unnatural' — what is needed is that learners be given the opportunity to make their own subconscious selection of items based on what they found communicatively useful at each stage of their development.

The materials can be used as a stimulus for acquisition when following conditions are met:

1. The success of enterprise generated by the materials must be demonstrated by the outcome and not by the process of the activity.
2. The focus of the enterprise must be on the message throughout, rather than on the channel, *i.e.*, the speaker must be concerned with what they have to say rather than how they are going to say it.
3. There must be an 'information gap' *i.e.*, one speaker must not know what the other speaker is going to say although at times he may be able to guess it.

The format of a number of good English textbooks of today is a result of a new awareness about language in general and the English language in particular. A lot of thinking and good deal of research in this area makes textbooks more or less relevant to the course intended. But in spite of much care, there are certain areas where our learners have difficulties with the materials.

These textbooks include both 'formal' and 'informal' styles of materials. But both are equally problematic for our learners. First one, because of difficult words, phrases, expressions, syntax and length of sentence used in the material; and the second one (informal), due to its colloquial expressions which our learners are not familiar with. The literary writings and essays that are prescribed for the Inter and first year BA (general/subsidiary/honours) courses appear (in many cases) too difficult for them not only in their language but also in their themes. Their language makes learning extremely difficult and slow. Their themes are unsuitable for the vast majority of our learners in view of the socio-cultural milieu they represent and the life they portray. Therefore, it promotes the dependency of learners on bazar notes or made-easy guides and hardly ever they read the original selection.

Prof. R. Quirk's (1963) remark on this issue is still valid today. He wrote, "Students who are scarcely able to read a restricted vocabulary text in modern standard English are expected to study a Shakespeare's play. Some of Jane Austin . . . . . . some of Pickwick papers at their most colloquial (not to mention *dialectal* and *archaic*) and sporadic poems from the 17th to the 19th C.".

It is found on observation that the average college learner of today is unprepared for the type of selections that are in use in this university. The teaching of English at school does not produce the essential skills and the necessary competence which are required for the use of English in colleges. They are like the beginners in arithmetic who want to learn the basic rules of addition and sub-traction or the multiplication tables. But what we offer them is calculus and trigonometry.

Textbooks used are not changed for a long time. The planners of courses have failed either to understand the need to concentrate on essentials or to provide for this need. This is partly due to the lack of awareness of what constitutes the essentials. The first essential to receive scholarly attention was the vocabulary, both content words and structural words. The second area which received scholarly attention includes the themes and their setting and the exercises and testing materials that are used in textbooks.

Insights in the choice of words depend upon two assumptions:

(a) Basic English; and
(b) Frequency counts.

Basic English is a miniature language that is claimed to have the range and utility of the 'whole English language'. It has 850 head words with rules for putting them to use. But the complexities of the grammatical system of basic English, depending on phrasal verbs, use of the same words as different parts of speech, compounding of free forms to its extensive use of metaphor etc, make it unsuitable for textbook materials or for classroom use, unless handled by experts.

Frequency based word-lists suffer from a number of limitations. In most cases, it is not the number of words that one comes across that matters as much as the guilty of one's mastery over them. It is not whether we know a word, but how we know it, which matters. It is not the quality of our understanding of them which matters. Therefore, how we learn words and how well we learn them are more important than the number of words we know. Like coins, real value of a word depends on several factors which keep changing. A FLS who attempts to use words which he has not fully assimilated for purposes of use in real life communication is worse off than one who, with comparatively fewer words to use, is able to use them effectively to convey his meaning.

Situations of use often determine the type of words that should be included at a particular stage in language teaching and in teaching materials. Words belong to situations of use and they get their meanings from these situations. So more often it is the theme that decides the choice of a particular set of words. Obviously, it is the sentence that lends a particular word its peculiar meaning – the meaning that is relevant to the situation it has been used in. Each situation that we choose to discuss will have its own accompanying vocabulary and frequent words will only form a part, in some case as very small part, of the total. Since in conversation there are a large number of situations, learners feel bewildered and it is not possible to include all the structural words in a particular class. Palmer's observation (1962) is very significant:

> "English contains about 20,000 words in fairly current use of these about 1,000 present considerable difficulty partly due to their importance and partly because of the number of meanings each of them convey. These prevent SL students in the early stages from using English correctly and effectively."

These difficult words include what are known as 'structure words' (which help us make the meaning of sentences clear). These words include the prepositions, conjunctions, the pronouns, the auxiliary verbs, the determiners, the negative particles, the interrogative adverbs and the adverbs of degree. These are less than 200 of these structure words in English. But most of them are very frequent and important in speech and writing. Miller (1951) finds that "the articles, prepositions, conjunctions, pronouns and auxiliary verbs determine the general form of statements, while the nouns, adjectives, adverbs and verbs contribute the content. The different forms repeat themselves more often than do the different contents, and so the minor parts of speech compose the major part of our utterances". Structure words have no definable meanings of their own, but help establish links and give meanings to sentences. Though small in number, they constitute the heart of the language. Hence there is a need to use them with great care. The question arises – do these structure words have any relevance for language teaching materials being prepared for and used in colleges?

Structure words clearly need primary attention even where learners come to college with five years of English in schools. Only a small number of these words, and in only a few of their senses, can be taught in our ordinary classrooms. The great bulk of them will require planned teaching in colleges. In reality, we find that even our teachers or textbook writers do not have an idea about the relevance of these structure words. In writing a textbook content words have got importance and structure words have either less or no importance in teaching learners vocabulary. In teaching English there is no emphasis on teaching these words if any; its use is limited to the teaching of prepositional phrases only.

Apart from word selection there are other assumptions which play an important role in the production of materials. Spread of psychological insight into human behaviour affects language teaching. Michael West (1926) proposed that a textbook ought to have mental age to correspond with the chronological age of the learners. The content of the book also corresponds to the interest of the learners. Most of the young learners dislike what is unnecessarily trivial or dry and commonplace. Materials that restrict them to the narrow world of the classroom, chalk and duster would not retain their interest.

To prepare teaching materials for school/college classes authors make use of literature. A typical general course is about the lives and adventures of imaginary characters. This type of content motivates and entertains the students. But the content itself doesn't have any communicative activity in the real sense. Its events and problems do not correspond to problems found outside the classroom. However good our teaching exercise or syllabus appear on paper, it is in the minds of the learners that they succeed or fail, says Cook (1983). Students' expectations are one of the important factors in the selection of teaching items. Materials provided to our learners do not correspond to the students' expectations and fail to motivate them.

A major source of content in the classroom are the students themselves. They had experiences of life, they have opinions and ideas of their own. But we cannot rely much on it due to certain shortcomings (Cook 1983). There are a large number of options to base our content upon but we should not restrict the content to conventional, fictional or alien contents only. The selection must correspond to the overall goals of the course-end and the psychological make-up of the learners as well as to build up the communicative skills in them.

The preparing of teaching materials involves age placement as well as other important factors, namely:

(a) Socio-cultural setting;
(b) The geography, the climate, the social and natural environment the learners inhabit; and
(c) Adequate exposition of the specialist concepts discussed or referred to.

Learning a language involves the learning of skills. For a long time it was thought that teaching materials were used to teach all aspects of language and all its skill simultaneously and there is hardly any provision for individual skills or sub-skills. But today linguists believe that speech was of primary and writing of secondary importance. Therefore, teaching materials with dialogues and exercises are included in the list of teaching items. In practical terms, in order to develop a particular skill we must concentrate our attention and effort on that skill and its sub-skills and exclusion of others which are not attainable in the given situation. The important factors to be considered in devising teaching materials are:

(a) Initial behaviour or entrance behaviour (EB);
(b) Desired terminal behaviour (DTB);
(c) Society's expectation of learner;
(d) Knowledge of classroom circumstances where the material will be used, namely, number of students, equipments used for teaching;
(e) Quality of teachers;
(f) Motivation of learners; and
(g) Size and strength of the class.

All such variables greatly influence the presentation of teaching materials. On the basis of survey conducted (Chapter 4), we find that a learner's initial behaviour does not correspond to the desired initial behaviour which is required for the admission in a particular class. Therefore, the materials catered for a specific initial 'behaviour' of learners proves to be problematic for the learners. A well prepared text (NCERT textbook) proves to be futile in our classroom due to large number of unmotivated students and lack of necessary equipments even in most popular of the schools, including government schools. In many schools even blackboard is not available. Classroom situations even in colleges have so many variables that it is impossible to make proper use of the prescribed teaching materials for language teaching.

Chaudhary (1990) also finds that teaching of English in almost all schools and colleges is still generally textbook centred. The entire emphasis is on teaching comprehension and appreciation of whatever verse or prose pieces might be prescribed for the particular course, besides very conventional kinds of essay, precis, paragraph and substance writing. There is no provision for teaching different skills like listening, speaking, reading and writing for less formal purposes. Consequently, learners find it absolutely difficult to express even ordinary things in English. Different publications introduce a series of textbooks meant for different levels of learners. They claim it to be "a complete language course". The textbook series produced by NCERT have also the same criteria of selection of the items and a teacher is expected to teach through the texts and exercises based thereon. But at college level, these specifications or grading of teaching items are not found. The rationale for the items in these books mostly lie in the mysterious whims and caprices of the members of the boards of studies. In L.N.M. University, Darbhanga, Bihar, these textbooks, mostly anthologies of English essays and poems, or short stories and one act plays by well-known writers are "literacy" pieces, without proper projection of the language contents. It is so with the Council of Intermediate Education too.

A brief list of anthologies and textbooks of different kinds prescribed indicates the ideas of the syllabus designers:

At intermediate Level

(1) Five one act play by A. Thakur

(2) Tales old and new – edited by R.C. Maxwell

or

Lamb's Tales from Shakespeare edited by C.K. William

(3) Intermediate English Prose and Poetry Selections published by Bihar Intermediate Education Council, Macmillan India Ltd.

BA. Part I level

(a) *General*

1. *Poetry:* The Siren's Song (ed) David Murdech
2. *Comedy*: Arms and the Man – G.B. Shaw

3. Grammar
4. Prosody

(b) *Honours*

1. History of literature
2. Individual authors
3. History of English language
4. Palgrave's Golden Treasury (OUP) edited by John Press
5. Mac Flecknoe – John Dryden
6. Lamia – Keats

(c) *Subsidiary*

1. New Golden Treasury edited by R.C. Prasad and M.Q. Towhee
2. The Silver Box – John Galsworthy
3. Grammar

(d) *B.A./B.Sc. (Pass & Hons) language paper*

1. Poems old and new edited by A. Thakur
2. Grammar

BA, Part II

(a) *General*

1. An anthology of short stories edited by Damodar Thakur
2. Romeo and Juliet – Shakespeare
3. Grammar and composition

(b) *Honours*

1. Edward II – Marlowe
2. Twellth Night – Shakespeare
   Macbeth – Shakespeare
3. The Rivals – Sheridan
4. English Essayists edited by S.K. Sinha (OUP)
5. Wuthering Heights – Emily Bronte
6. The Mayor of Casterbridge – Thomas Hardy
7. Modern Short Stories – II Series (OUP)

(c) *Subsidiary*

1. The Oldman and the Sea—Earnest Hemingway
2. Grammar

BA. Part III (Honours)

1. *Paper V:* History of Criticism – 16th to 20th Century
   (a) General trends

(b) Individual authors
(c) T.S. Eliot – three essays introduced by S.K. Kumar (OUP)

2. *Paper VI:* Modern literature
(a) 20th Century verse – An Anglo-American Anthology edited by C.T. Thomas (Macmillan)
(b) Candida – G.B. Shaw
(c) Where Angles Fear to gread – E.M. Foster

3. *Paper VII*
(a) Indian Poetry in English — Pd. Hari Mohan Prasad and Chakradhar Pd. Singh (Sterline Pub.)
(b) Untouchable – Mulk Raj Anand
(c) An Anthology of Indian English Prose – edited by R.C. Prasad and J.P. Singh (Motilal Banarasi Das)
(C_1) Essays
(C_2) Stories

4. *Paper VIII: 4.1. American literature*
(a) Twentieth C. Verse – An Anglo-American Anthology edited by C.T. Thomas (Macmillan)
(b) Farewell to Arms – Earnest Hemingway
(c) Death of a Salesman – Arthur Miller (Panguin Pub)

4.2 *Linguistics*
Sec. I – Definition of language and linguistics
Sec. II – Speech mechanism, phonemes and word formation. Structural morphology and structural syntax.

4.3 *Essays*
(i) Literary essays
(ii) General essays

After having a look at the items prescribed, one fact is obvious that in presenting these items there is hardly any emphasis on any particular skill and the teaching items are not conducive to the development of communicative skills to even advanced (Hons) level learners of English. Prof. Amrik Singh (1984), a teacher and educational administrator of considerate repute, has found the drafting of the syllabus in most disciplines as "both unscientific and unacademic".

Ranjtha (1983) finds English, used as a teaching language at the undergraduate level, had distinctive grammatical and lexical choices. Our materials are from a typical classroom settings. One teacher and a number of students willing to listen to the teacher. The teacher imports knowledge/information through a combination of lecture and questions. The latter employed to ascertain how far the students have understood the 'lecture'. Very often our teaching ends with presenting the teaching items. At college level most of the teachers think that establishments of these items is not worth bothering about. It is thought to be students' liability and very often students write English only for their examinations. This last step is an integral part in the entire process and questions and exercises are framed for the repetition of the teaching item. This part is neglected due to many reasons such as weight of syllabus, problem of time, etc.

The degree of formality in the classroom ranges between the level that characterises highly formal discourse (public speech) and informal speech (as in conversation), but a mean is more or less maintained so that the discourse does not plunge into high informality even when the teacher is inclined to feel one with the participants or the topic changes to something personal or contextual.

Structures presented in the classroom, though planned in advance, often deviate from the set pattern for a variety of reasons – doubts expressed by students, spontaneous ideas coming to the mind of the teacher, his/her memory limitations and other unexpected disturbances. Code switching or switching of the tone is used to achieve special effects. In the actual classroom situation in higher classes we find that the choice made by the teacher is often individualistic because of the unevenness of the Entry Level Behaviour of students with diverse educational backgrounds. This puts a peculiar constraint on the performance of a teacher.

Fig 2.5 shows, quantitatively, the relative occurrence of the various structures. It is clear from the graph that initial behaviour of students at undergraduate level is not upto the level which is desired at the entrance in colleges. The marks obtained by them did not correspond to their entrance behaviour and the result is a complete failure of the teaching materials which is designed for them.

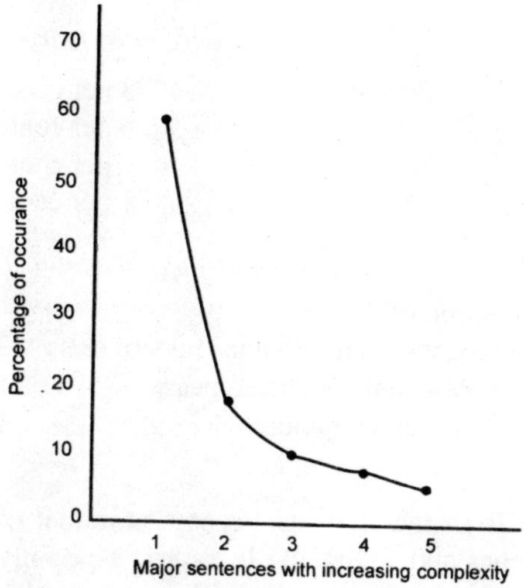

Fig. 2.5: Major Sentences with increasing Complexity

Note: Variables
1. Simple, SP, SPO, SPC, SPA; 2. Simple SPCA, SPOA; 3. Compound; 4. Complex; 5. Mixed
S – Subject; P - Verbal group; O – Object; C – Complement; A – Adverbial
Source: Adopted form unpublished M. Phil. Dissertation, Ranjtha 1983, JNU Delhi

At the time of offering English at undergraduate level, our students were very enthusiastic and in the class their attitude towards lessons had been more ambivalent. To develop a better understanding of how they feel about studying literature, they had been given some questions:

1. Which literary genres were most favoured or feared by them.
2. Which aspect of literature gave them most trouble.

Following table shows their response according to priority.

Response 1 : The genre most enjoyed

Novel	—	44 per cent
Short story	—	43 per cent
Drama	—	7 per cent
Poetry	—	5 per cent

Response 2 : The genre most feared

Poetry	—	73 per cent
Drama	—	20 per cent
Novel	—	7 per cent
Short story	—	1 per cent

Response 3 : Aspects causing particular trouble

Interpretation of theme	41 per cent
Vocabulary, especially in non-modern texts	27 per cent
Cultural/philosophical differences	12 per cent
Literary style and structure	11 per cent
Others	9 per cent

What emerges from the students' responses is that they have many fears and anxieties about studying literature, especially poetry. These fears are based partly on their lack of background knowledge and partly on a certain mystique about literature. This investigation reveals an overwhelming preference for prose fiction, with an equally overwhelming distaste for poetry.

We teach poetry in terms of its content and learner's attention is focused not on the collection of linguistic features but on aesthetic features. But in a language class or in a communicative classroom poetry offers an interesting colloquialism or features of style. In terms of O'Conner and Arnold (1977), a high rise in the question would be suitable for a casual query; whilst a high unstressed prehead followed by a low rise could indicate incredulous amusement. In linguistic terms, poetry is deviation from the norms of the language. These may be:

(a) Phonological
(b) Lexical
(c) Syntactic
(d) Semantic
(e) Stylistic
(f) Register mixing

But these deviations are meant for emphasizing certain point of view and reflect a sophisticated use of language for better achievements. Therefore, it could be studied by pin-pointing the linguistic features.

Apart from these pedagogical and psychological factors, there are some non-linguistic factors which affect proper material production to a great extent. These non-academic factors are:

1. Price and availability factor;
2. Spurious textbooks and notes;
3. Pressures of publishers and others;
4. Projection of the bias and prejudices;
5. Model questions available; and
6. Use of unfair means in examinations.

We find that problem lies (starts) right from the syllabus design to the availability of textbooks. Even if the board of study is fair and aware of the needs of standard textbooks and prescribes 'standard publications' most of the time, it proves futile due to the factors mentioned above. Due to prescription of model questions and use of unfair means, students' attitude towards standard text is negative. Spurious locally manufactured materials with notes and prepared answers on much lower rates than the original ones encourage students to bypass the prescribed texts. These hurriedly prepared 'books' were written on commercial point of view. Hence they are full of mistakes and misprints and the exercise materials are left out in favour of readymade answers.

For a long time the use of these softwares (books) cater to the conventional pattern of teaching. But pioneering works have been done over the years in the field of ELT which are clearly outside the established tradition. For several important reasons self-teaching materials: Software (books, maps, charts etc) and hardware equipments (tape recorder, video, slides, projectors, language labs. etc.) are available to cater to individual needs, ability and speed. Programmed learning and materials related to its theory and principles appear to be a promising development in this connection. Even media of the electronic age brings awareness and enlightenment in the field of learning and teaching in ELT. Many of our schools, however, do not have minimum basic materials like blackboard and chalk. So, we have to depend for a long time to come, on the conventional teaching materials. Therefore, there is an urgent need to update the teaching methodology.

Methodology

Chomsky (1957) does not view language primarily as a conventional symbol system concerned with communication or co-operation between people. He defines it to be a set (finite or infinite) of sentences each finite in length and constructed out of a finite set of elements'. This is a definition in terms of structure rather than function. But the relationship between structure and function is central issue in contemporary linguistics (for details please see Chomsky, 1965).

The concept of communicative competence has been discussed by a range of scholars – Jakobovits (1970), Habermas (1970), Hymes (1971) and Savignon (1972). The literature on communicative competence has been surveyed by various writers with varying emphasis (Le Page 1975, Munby 1978, Canale and Swain 1980). Applied linguists agreed to specify as clearly as possible not only the formal features of linguistic system but the ways in which these formal features may legitimately be operated. For language teachers there have been attempts to define the dimensions of language use from a number of different directions.

Language teaching, most of us hold, involves a conscious, even painstaking application of rules, in which constructing a sentence is consciously planned and publicly explicable. In order to attain a high level of potential fluency by orthodox, self conscious learning, *e.g.*, those who have learnt a language from a "teach yourself book", their language use must be limited to what they have encountered in natural circumstances. To overcome this problem, Krashen (1982) suggests that teachers put their students to extensive reading which constitutes normal input, but here again there are problems in determining the relations between the struggling through a book in a SL with a dictionary and occasional recourse to a grammar. In fact, one cannot use a language if one cannot produce automatic appropriate responses in handling the language. Brumfit (1984) says that it is merely descriptive with no explanatory powers, we cannot justifiably use it as a basis for language teaching methodology. The teaching needs an increasing awareness and demands to produce work for display. Language display for evaluation tends to lead to concern for accuracy, monitoring, reference rules, possibly explicit knowledge, problem solving and evidence of skill getting. In contrast, language use requires fluency, expression rules, a reliance on implicit knowledge and automatic performance. It will, on occasions, require monitoring and problem solving strategies, where the students produce. The teacher corrects and the student tries again. But due to other factors discussed elsewhere in this chapter, the desired goal is not reached.

The emphasis is on the accuracy/fluency of the learner. If the language is being produced for display purposes, the learner is intended to produce examples of language according to the requirements of the teacher, who may be demanding phonological, syntactical, lexical, functional, or stylistic convergence on a norm which may or may not have been specified. Whatever the conditions, the learner is expected to demonstrate usage, not use (Widdowson, 1978a) and will adopt strategies accordingly. If such strategies are inappropriate for some or all of the activities involving natural language use, their encouragement in the classroom needs careful justification. At the same time, the arguments for a .substantial proportion of the time being spent on activities which do involve natural language-use require careful examination also. Due to factors like time spent, knowledge and willingness of the teacher and so on language teaching is not very successfully performed.

Brumfit (1984) says the language is frequently taught as a code without the potential activity. This takes as well beyond the capacities of conventional needs-analysis, for need-analysis has operated passively as a sociolinguistic tool, without relating itself to the normal, intellectual or aesthetic needs, Munby (1978) says that the teaching of general English or French, or any other language cannot be 'directly derivable from the prior identification of the communication needs of that particular participant or participant stereotype', except when learners have prestable and stable needs.

Rod Ellis (1982) puts it: "A methodology will encourage acquisition and must ensure that the learner is left free to find his own route; it must be facilitative rather than prescriptive".

In language teaching there is a great confusion between content and methods. So first of all it should be resolved. In Hirst's (1974) view "If a curriculum is a plan of activities at achieving objectives, it is a plan involving two other elements, a content to be used and a method to be employed to bring about learning".

The content will have a varying relationship to the objectives of teaching, depending on needs, it has been chosen. Content in practice gives a context for the development of certain abilities, but except when we view learning as simply the accumulation of 'facts'. Anthony (1963) says the methods are 'types of activities' or what in language teaching have come to be called 'techniques'. According to Hirst (1974), content has to be related to our choice of objectives, both long-term and short-term, and 'methods' have to be related to the kinds of interaction we choose.

The process of learning is complicated, but in order to facilitate it, different forms of thought must be distinguished and this can only be done 'by reference to the particular set of terms and relations, which each of the distinct forms of thought employ. These thoughts need to be examined by means of a logical sequence, but it is not necessary to claim that there is only one logical sequence for each of them. The role of methodologist is to describe and explore the range of possible options available to teachers in as principled a way as possible, as Johnson and Morrow (1981) observe. In an ideal language course it should be possible to see a set of precise objectives in terms of which the classroom procedures and the techniques, which the teacher uses to implement them, have been structured and applied. The mere adoption of a notional or functional syllabus does not guarantee that we are going to teach our students to communicate. Functions are expressed through elements of the language system; in other words a functional course is ultimately concerned with language forms – just as a grammatically based course is. The difference may lie simply in the way the forms are organised. But communication involves much more that simply a knowledge of forms; it depends crucially on the ability to use forms in appropriate ways. The problem with most first generation 'functional' textbooks is that they have concentrated too much on setting out forms – not enough on practising communication.

There are certain underlying principles by which teachers can judge procedures as to whether their overall aims of teaching have been worth adopting or not. Every lesson should be an operation of some kind which the student might actually want to perform in the foreign language. In reading, he might be understanding a set of instructions; in writing it might be a letter reserving accommodation at a hotel, in listening it might be understanding a set of instructions and so on. All these operations can be approached on a variety of different levels of sophistications. Learning the question of the third person singular after present tense on page 23 of the textbook is one thing; learning it so that one can ask questions at a railway station (Does this train go to Delhi? Does it stop at Lucknow? etc.) is quite other. But here the problem that very few teachers know now to choose an appropriate procedure to teach a particular structural item. They stick to the age-old tradition of presenting structural items in such a way that a learner thinks he has to master only that particular structural item given on a particular page. They don't see any further implication of that item and they don't have any drill to consolidate that item. Teachers are either unable or unwilling to coordinate that particular structural item to their (student's) day-to-day communicative demands. In fact, every item should be open-ended and should enable the learner to see clearly that he can use that particular item in his daily life in several ways and in different situations. He can see it contributing to the performance of some real and specific task in the foreign language. The teacher and student both should be aware of the fact they are doing. But both of them do not see the above mentioned facts. They only stick to the textbooks because they are examined for that particular line given in the textbook. Therefore, the focus of every lesson (or part of lesson) should be on performing of some operation – learning how to do something.

Communication is a dynamic and developing phenomenon so it cannot easily be analysed into component features without its nature being destroyed in the process. It is, of course, possible to identify various formal ways language is used communicatively and these can be studied individually. But in communication what is needed is the ability to deal with strings of sentences and ideas and in the oral modes (speaking and listening) these strings must be processed in what is called 'real time'. When one is conversing with somebody, one cannot study what they say at length before producing an appropriate reply; the whole process must be instantaneous. In handling English in the classroom, in fact here we do the same thing. We teach our students by explaining the text bit by bit in a similar fashion. In doing so the fluency and the essence of the language is severely hampered. Our students cultivate this analytic habit and attempt to know each and every word of the target language and they find communication extremely difficult and their communicative ability is severely hampered. In written mode also it is not advisable to produce individual elements of the message. What is needed is the ability to work in the context of the whole. Thus a crucial feature of a communicative method will be that it operates with stretches of language above the sentence level, and operates with real language in real situations.

A method which aims to develop the ability of students to communicate in SL will aim to replicate, as far as possible, the process of communication, so the practice of the forms of the target language can take place within a communicative framework. The concept of "information gap" is one of the most fundamental element in communicative teaching. Any exercise or procedure should be considered in its light and teacher's job is to setting up situations where information gaps exist and to motivate the students to bridge them in appropriate ways (for details please see K. Johnson and K. Morrow 1981).

In communication the information, which is transferred, is of the 'interpersonal' (social) type rather than 'ideational' (factual), (*see* Haliday 1973), whereas in classroom an information gap exercise means that one student or teacher must be in a position to tell another something that the second student does not already know. Here lies the cause of interference in the communication classroom situation. In classroom the student's transfer of information is limited to the facts (content) of the lesson and not to the interactional aspect of the language.

Students are generally exposed to the exercises controlled in language use. Therefore there are always doubts in the listeners' mind about what is to come next. They must not only choose the ideas they want to express at a given moment, but also what linguistic forms are appropriate to express them. Deciding on these under the severe time pressure which language use involves, is one of the main problem of our learners. They find themselves helpless when they have to perform certain functions in an uncontrolled situation.

In real life, one person speaks to another because he wishes to invite him, to threaten him, or to reassure him and this aim will be in his mind all the time he is speaking. What he says to the other person will be designed to reach that aim, and what the other person says to him will be evaluated in terms of that aim. That means what a man says to somebody depends not only on what he has just said to the other but also on what he wants to get out of the conversation. The strategies and tactics involved in using language in this way are of fundamental importance in communication. These strategies and tactics are left out of account in classroom teaching.

Today emphasis shifts from teaching to learning and learning becomes, to a large extent, the learner's responsibility. The teacher can help, advise and teach; but only the learner can learn. Here the activities demand an environment where doing things is possible. In a classroom where students sitting under the strict-eyed teacher, critically evaluating students' performance, destroys all hope of communication. The students have problems in combining activity with discipline but a cardinal tenet of learning theory is that one learns to do by only practising communicative activities we can learn to communicate. But this does not mean that the teacher can just sit back and let the students get on with it. The learning should be structured within a framework and the provision of this framework is largely the responsibility of the teacher. The learners must be free to do what they want to do, but they must be structured within a framework.

In Bihar, including Darbhanga, classrooms are teacher-oriented; students sitting in rows and the teacher delivering lectures. The learners have hardly any scope of participation in the teaching-learning process. Students only give answers to the questions asked and there is not enough time to practise that particular function. The practice and production side get very little time in proportion to the presentation. It is often said that a communicative approach to the language teaching encourages students to make mistakes, particularly of grammar. The conventional language teaching methods aim at eradicating mistakes by tightly controlling what the learner is allowed to say. When these controls are removed and learners are encouraged to start using the language with all that this involves, then from a certain point of view problems are bound to arise; but these problems are not solved by an approach which insists on former accuracy at the expense of use. It may well be that it will require the flexibility to treat different things as 'mistakes' at different stages in the learning process.

Communication involves using appropriate forms in appropriate ways. The acquisition of forms is, therefore, a central part of language learning and learning-teaching can be divided into two phases – learning the forms and then learning to use them.

Before proceeding towards evaluating the methods, it is important to know about objectives behind it. Every teacher has a particular objective in his mind when he is going to teach. According to that objective he adopts certain methods. W.M. Rivers (1968) says that we find each one of them has a different combination and priority of objectives in mind and accordingly they choose widely different techniques for achieving those objectives. There are so many approaches to language teaching suggested by scholars. They had different approaches to language, keeping in mind a particular aspect of language. In brief, we just view their attitude towards teaching methodology. Those objectives are as follows:

(a) To develop student's intellectual powers through SL study,
(b) To increase the student's personal culture through the study of great literature and philosophy,
(c) To increase the student's understanding of how language functions and bring him to a greater awareness of the functioning of his own language,
(d) To teach the student to read the SL with comprehension so that he may keep abreast of modern writing, research and information,
(e) To bring the student to a greater understanding of people across national barriers, and
(f) To provide the student with skills which will enable him to communicate orally and, to some degree, in writing.

As we see, the last four of the aims listed above are the most relevant for today's student at the secondary level. In last few decades there has been increase in research into the language and the interest of many in second language teaching.

The grammar based approach has several drawbacks although one has to admit, it was not without its success. There is no doubt that many students did learn and master the language and managed to achieve a degree of fluency in it, but examining them closely it is clear that it could be attributed to some other factors also. Perhaps some of the teachers had unconsciously adopted 'direct' practices or else some of the students had been exposed to communicative situation. The grammar-based approach, however, with its focus on the purely formal aspects of the language stresses linguistic items and does not take into consideration other aspects like semantics and pragmatics which are recognised as the more important aspects of language hence it presents a limited approach to language learning. Very often the student can cite all the grammar rules but is unable to produce even a single error free sentence.

Another difficulty is to decide how much grammar to teach. It would be an impossible task to deal with whole of it. This approach sees language as a system, and language position as consisting of mastery of that system; the grammar is context free.

The other area of conflict is between the grammatical presentation of items, where forms, which are governed by similar rules, are grouped together but in their pedagogic presentation they would need to be demonstrated in combination with other forms, for example, questions should not be taught in isolation from statements as in daily communication they are invariably used together.

In the early twentieth century itself, however, approaches to the teaching of English have begun to change. Harold Palmer (1964) defines language learning as "a habit forming process". He spoke in favour of repetitive drills and felt that learning grammar rules, their knowledge had no compatibility with competence in the language. His contention is that it is totally unnecessary and superfluous to explain the rules of the language. The only purpose such explanations serve is to satisfy the curiosity of the student, but they do not help us form new habits, they do not develop automation. During the World War-I, a programme for Army was devised by the American descriptive linguists in forties. The designing, organising and production of materials for these language classes were very successful and it was probably due to intensive communicative sessions.

Audiolingualism is the new teaching methodology which emphasised the teaching of oral skills derived both from the Army language course and from structural theories which were based on the findings of the behavioural psychologists. In it the learner is taken through a sequence of stimulus-response circumstances which bring him nearer to the projected aim, that of building up speech habits. Instead of learning the rules of grammar of the language, the emphasis shifted to practice and hence it was not thought necessary to know or to understand the rules of grammar of the language they were studying.

The classroom activities, as suggested by Krashan (1977), were to consist of:

(a) new material, both lexical and grammatical, presented in the form of dialogue which were to represent pieces of real communication;

(b) a series of pattern drills in which the structures and vocabulary introduced in the dialogue would be manipulated until the structures became unconscious habits for the students; and

(c) a recombination response material in which the student tried to apply the newly acquired structure in semi free conversations.

But due to certain reasons, it did not achieve the kind of success. It is felt that the total emphasis on oral skills leads to frustration since by banning the written word it took much longer to learn a language and mother tongue interference too could not be eradicated. The drills become mechanical and hence monotonous; since it sees language acquisition as a purely mechanistic process and not a cognitive one. While practising drills, there is no understanding either of the sense of the sentence or of rules they embodied.

The dissatisfaction with structural materials was reinforced by developments in psychology, which shifted from behaviourist explanations of learning to a cognitive and mentalist approach. In language teaching it is again a return to grammar-explanation followed by various sorts of exercise to practice the rule in question. (Krashen 1977). The emphasis was on a conscious understanding of the rule being practiced. Since they do not abandon the drill format of the structralists and hence there is not much scope for the students to create or use language that the already know.

The communicative methodology, based on a notional approach to language teaching, moved away from the teaching of grammar rules and structural patterns to the presentation of 'problem solving' situations where the student would be forced to communicate and in the process produce the appropriate response. It is felt that in using the language for a number of communicative functions like making enquiries, asking for directions, polite social conversation which the student will unconsciously absorb the rules. But what is apparent here that it is not essentially different in approach from the earlier structuralist approach.

By 'functionalism' we mean a view of language as a dynamic open system by means of which members of community exchange information. It grows out of research in psycholinguistics and sociolinguistics and new theories of descriptive linguistics which reveal in increasing importance of semantics and this led the descriptive linguistics to accept that part of the meaning of a word or a sentence lies in the situation in which it is used.

Notional syllabuses are radically different from earlier

approaches because of their sociolinguistic base and they have their roots in the functional approach. Earlier courses had a grammatical pedagogic organisation, therefore, it is important to decide on "...what basis we will select the language to which the learner will be exposed and which we will expect him to acquire.

All approaches whether grammatical, structuralist or functional as belonging to two conceptually distinct types of approaches which may be synthetic or analytic. A synthetic language teaching strategy is one in which the different parts of language are taught separately and step by step so that acquisition is a process of gradual accumulation of these parts until the whole structure of language has become built up. But in analytical approaches, there is no attempt at linguistic control of the learning environment. Much greater variety of linguistic structure is permitted and the learner's task is to approximate his own linguistic behaviour more and more closely to the global language. The notional syllabus is an embodiment of this approach. The advantage of the notional syllabus is that it takes the communicative facts of language into account from the beginning without losing sight of grammatical and situational factors. It is potentially superior to the grammatical syllabus it will produce a communicative competence and because its evident concern with the use of language will sustain the motivation of the learners.

In the last two decades the emphasis in language teaching has shifted more and more to the learner's acquiring a communicative competence in the language rather than a knowledge of its forms and structures. Debates and arguments have spoken strongly in favour of fluency over accuracy and use versus usage (Brumfit 1984, Widdowson 1983). Syllabus planners also have become much more concerned about the needs and requirements of the learners and feel that it is essential to take these factors into account: "Are learners aiming for a general or a specialised language competence? Is the course extensive or intensive? Is it a short- or a long-term course? Is the ultimate goal some limited proficiency in the language or is it intended to proceed until native like proficiency is achieved? Are the learners adult or children? The answers to these and other questions will influence the precise form that the syllabus takes and will change the weighting of different criteria that might be used", (Wilkinson 1979).

His reasoning that a focus on the semantic rather than grammatical aspects of language will bring about more effective learning.

None of these, however, rejects outright the earlier grammatical approach. What they rather suggest is that the best method would be a combination of the various approaches depending upon the needs of the students and their suitability for them.

William Littlewood (1981) develops the implications of adopting a communicative approach on these two fundamental postulates:

1. A communicative approach opens up a wider perspective as language. In particular, it considers language not only in terms of its structures (grammar and vocabulary), but also in terms of the communicative functions that it performs.
   In other words, we begin to look not only at language forms, but also at what people do with these forms when they want to communicate with each other. For example, the form 'why don't you close the door' might be used for a number of communicative purposes such as asking a question, making a suggestion or issuing an order.
   We can, therefore, combine the newer functional view of language with the traditional structural view in order to achieve a more complete communicative perspective. This enables us to give a fuller account of what students have to learn in order to use language as a means of communication. It also suggests an alternative basis for selecting and organizing the language items that we need to teach.
2. A communicative approach opens up a wider perspective on language learning. In particular, it makes one more strongly aware that it is not enough to teach learners how to manipulate the structures of the SL. They must also develop strategies for relating these structures to their communicative functions in real situations and real time.
   Littlewood (1981) says that it is, therefore, important to provide learners with ample opportunities to use the language themselves for communicative purposes. It must also be remembered that teachers are ultimately concerned with developing the learners' ability to take part in the process of communicating through language rather than their perfect mastery of individual structures (though this may still be a useful step towards the broader goal).

The principles underlying communicative approach and in the first language acquisition are as follows:

(a) The initial focus will be on understanding the language as it is seen in babies—that they are capable of understanding much more than they can produce in complete sentences.
(b) Production is elicited in gradual steps and, therefore, no pressure is exerted on the students to make them speak before they have built up confidence in their ability to do so.
(c) Grammatical errors are ignored at least to begin with as correction may block learning: the emphasis is on communication.
(d) The syllabus is devised around communicative topics and not grammatical categories as the goal at the beginning: comprehension and production levels are to generate communicative acquisition.
(e) The activities which are organised in the classroom must encourage an atmosphere which is free of anxiety and which can be brought about by a cordial relationship between the teacher and the students and among the students themselves through the selection of activities which are appropriate, relevant and stimulating.

What implications do all these developments in language teaching methodology have for Indian students? William Littlewood (1981) in his introduction notes the needs of the learner as described in the council of Europe's 'Threshold Level', "people who want to prepare themselves in a general way to be able to communicate socially on straightforward everyday matters with people from other countries who came their way, and to be get round and lead a reasonably normal life when they visit another country". These goals are obviously appropriate only for a small minority of Indian students and hence it would be unrealistic to adopt it as a goal for all the students. With government policy and the educationists arguing in favour of continuing English in its role for academic goal would be to chalk out those spheres where English is necessary and accordingly concentrate on the skills that would be required.

We have already examined the school and college syllabus which record the awareness for the development of communicative skill, but the benefits never accrue to students because the approach has remained unchanged.

In the Indian situation what has been observed is that even when textual material is used, the texts are seen only as a means to master and drill the form of the language. At the college level, where literary texts are introduced, the focus is on the critical study of style and other literary aspects to enable the students to critically evaluate the text that is being taught. However, neither of these syllabuses succeeds in producing in the students an ability to comprehend what they are reading or to produce relatively error-free sustained efforts. The result is that these syllabuses have fostered a dependence on bazaar notes and cramming. It is essential to formulate a syllabus that will rather encourage independence and confidence and a shift in orientation to a communicative approach which, it is felt, will be successful since the functionally oriented language teacher attempts to analyse, synthesize and teach dynamic discourse rather than the decontextualised sentence (Bell & Horper 1978).

The advantages of adopting the communicative method are considerable. Bell has clearly enunciated the shift in the emphasis that has taken place. Meaning is now in the forefront of the syllabus designer's mind and learning a language is now seen as learning how to mean in a wide range of social settings. The emphasis on meaning has had the effect or concentrating attention on the needs of the learner and this, in turn, has given fresh impetus to the design of courses for specific, often job-related, purposes in contrast with the global orientation of earlier courses. In essence, a functional approach seeks to provide the learner not only with the linguistic knowledge which permits him to create and is important for the teacher to maintain a positive approach and to focus his attention approvingly on the learning that is taking place rather than concentrating on correcting errors and mistakes committed.

This is the dilemma of the teacher of English as summed up by Patnaik (1985), "The teacher of English in India is in a state of indecision on the issue of the variety of English which should acquire the status of the educational model. He is aware that the teaching of a foreign model like British English is a virtually impossible proposition, but he cannot opt for a home grown model like Indian English, because it is as yet undefined in a precise way and also because it lacks prestige at the moment". The strategy suggested by

B.N. Patnaik is to ignore and gloss over those deviant forms which are considered merely odd but not ungrammatical. The students must be cautioned about those forms which are inappropriate. For example, slang expressions should be discouraged.

It has been found that most of the materials based on communicative approach are unsuitable for Indian students from the point of view of the contexts in which they occur as they are generally European, British or American culture-specific, hence alien to majority of students. We, therefore, need to produce materials rooted in the Indian context in order to motivate the students by generating enthusiasm and interest over appropriately contextualised materials. Before doing this we have to answer certain questions about the role of English in India today and what specific skills would be needed by the students in order to effectively perform these functions.

After reviewing different approaches to teaching we find that none of the approaches is totally irrelevant. Rivers (1968) says that as we study the evolution of language teaching methods, we find that what is most effective in each method being taken up again at a later date, elaborate and refashioned, so that the best of the past is not lost but serves the purposes of the present. Therefore, no matter what method is in vogue or is officially advocated, the individual teacher who is professionally alert will adopt its techniques to his purposes, and to what he feels to be appropriate for the particular class he is teaching, having regard to their age level, their situation and their educational needs. Any method ceases to be efficient when it is applied inflexibly, according to set procedures in every situation. As Corder (1977) says the success of enterprise generated by the materials must be demonstrated by the outcome and not by the process of the activity. The focus of the enterprise must be on the message throughout, rather than on the channel.

In adopting any method a teacher should keep certain questions in mind:

(a) What are the objectives of the method.
(b) Whether these objectives are appropriate for the teaching.
(c) Whether the techniques advocated achieve the stated objectives in the most economical way.

(d) Whether these techniques maintain the interest and enthusiasm of the learners.
(e) Whether these techniques are appropriate for all types of students.
(f) And whether the demands, these techniques make on the teacher, are such that he can carry a full day's teaching load.

We had already gone through the contents of syllabus of undergraduate courses. But there is not any specific proposal for adaptation of methods. Therefore, every teacher had his own methods according to objectives he has in mind. Our evaluation system and question pattern forced them to adopt a critical approach to the items prescribed for students and oral aspect is totally neglected. If tests are conducted for oral skill they are also patterned on the content of the material prescribed, instead of their communicative ability. Their answer has formal discourse of a particular poet or writer. All these methods leads learners towards cramming of the content matter and they rush towards the bazaar notes. Therefore, whatever the methods adopted, they are not satisfactory for the development of learners' communicative ability. They do not have enough exposure to the language outside the classroom, so our learners have to totally depend on the classroom teaching.

J.A. Ranjtha (1983) in her study of English used in the classroom puts forward an argument for consideration of non-segmental phonological features, which play an important role in the teaching of language, which are:

(a) Pitch variation
(b) Variation in the loudness
(c) Variation in the speed
(d) Pause
(e) Hesitation
(f) Para-linguistic features

    (fa) Prior planning
    (fb) Deviation from the accepted pattern for a variety of reasons:
    Doubts expressed by students,
    Spontaneous ideas coming to the mind of the teacher,

His memory limitation,
Other unexpected disturbance

(fc) Repetition for fixing information for ensuring better comprehension, for clarity,

(fd) Redundancy: Superfluous or redundant words in language

(fe) Inter-sentence relationship

(ff) Sentence structure : at the undergraduate level, many people expect the teacher to use more complex, constructions involving subordinating in different ways. But in our classroom, the choice made by the teacher is quite different, especially when the teacher is performing expository or explanatory teaching. Apart from other reasons, the background from which students came from plays a great part in the choice of structures, since many of our students may not have an idea of basic sentence structure. This puts a peculiar constraint on the performance of a teacher.

Materials provided for our students are based on a description of what the learner is to acquire and are designed to focus on specific items of usage or use. Rod Ellis (1982) says, the conditions under which acquisition can take place will not have been met for the environment will be 'unnatural' and the route a prescribed one. What is needed is that the learners should be given the opportunity to make their own subconscious selection of items, based on what they find communicatively useful at each stage of their development. But this does not happen due to lack of time and enterprise. The success of enterprise must be demonstrated by the outcome instead of the process of the activity (Corder 1977). We are more concerned with the process of the activity and focus on the channel instead of message, what the learners have to say.

The question-answer method used in the classes such as given below:

"A – What is your name?
"B – Rohit Dev".

shows the success in the "process" not in the "product", as in many cases the students will already know each other's name. But if the focus is on the message, then the listeners have to copy the model provided. Since in the above example there is no information gap and certainly there will be no need for any further negotiation either of content or of language. But if the student is asked an open-ended question which evokes a number of answers from the part of learner, there is an obvious information gap, negotiation will be required whenever the teacher's message is not clear or listener fails to understand and he will need to call on a wide range of communicative resourcefulness from the part of teacher. In such circumstances our students find themselves helpless. They are taught only content of the subject matter and what is demanded of them is a critical appreciation of that particular prose or poetry piece. If someone is more concerned in their development, they put more importance to accuracy of structures rather than the message *i.e.*, what the learner wants to say.

Most of us hold the view that accuracy get priority over fluency: but one thing that is often forgotten is that in spoken language the conveyance of the message is of primary importance. If a message is successfully conveyed the communication is done. According to the argument presented by M. Swan (1985) it is not enough just to learn what is in the grammar and dictionary. There are two levels of meaning in language usage and use. Traditional courses taught one of these kinds of meaning but neglected the other.

When we described the grammatical meaning of a sentence, we have not accounted for the way it is used as an utterance, since there are things that are not conveyed by the grammar but are also understood. They too are governed by the 'rules' which are known to both speaker and learner. People who speak the same language share a communicative competence. But in ELT a learner has to learn rules of communication as well as rules of grammar (Wilkins 1976).

The sentences, "your coat's on the floor", might serve a number of communicative functions depending on the contextual or situational circumstances in which it was used. It is possible to learn a large number of sentence patterns and a large number of words which can fit into them without knowing how they are put to communicative use (Widdowson 1978). It is accurate grammatically but not communicatively. It may convey the message but not in the proper way. The 'rules of use' that determine how we interpret utterances such as Widdowson's sentence about the policeman are mostly non- language-specific and amount to little more than the operation of experience and commonsense. The precise value of an utterance is given by the interaction of its structural and lexical meaning with the situation in which it is used. Of course, cultures differ somewhat in their behaviour, and these differences are reflected in language. There are phrases and sentences in any language which conventionally carry intentional meanings that are not evident from their forms.

Structural dialogues lack communicative intent and one cannot identify what communicative operation the learner can engage in as a result of practice. The result of purely structural practice is the ability to produce a range of usage, but not the ability to use forms appropriately. Our interest is in the form, not on when and where to use it or what one achieves by using it. English notoriously has a wealth of colloquial, slang and taboo expressions. "There are rules of use without which the rules of grammar would be useless" (Johnson 1981).

Though we examine our students for comprehension skill which are not specifically taught, we leave that to their own reading. What is important in teaching comprehension skill is the art of prediction. Native listeners/readers make all sorts of predictions about the nature of what they are about to hear/read based on their knowledge of the subject, their familiarity with the speaker or writer and other relevant features (M. Swan 1985). If our students predict badly in a real life comprehensive task, it can only be for one or two reasons; either they lack essential background knowledge (of the subject matter or the interactional context), or their command of English language is not good enough. It needs to be emphasised that everyone, in any language, needs to develop the skills of adjustment and negotiation. Training in making intelligent guess will play an important part in learning to understand the spoken form of a foreign language (Brown 1977).

Our students feel difficulty in transferring skills from his or her mother tongue to the foreign language, it is needed to know why this skill is blocked. They seem to understand most of the words they hear but not really grasping the message. It is a matter of overload – the learner's command of the language is just fluent enough for him to decode the words and he has no processing capacity to spare for interpreting what he hears. It may be either due to lack of interest or because they have been trained to read texts in such a different way from 'real life' situations that they are unable to regard them as a piece of communication. This problem is caused by poor methodology and it is important that student should be exposed to appropriate sample of language and given relevant and motivating activities to help them to learn. A teacher must be facilitative rather than prescriptive. There are two crucial aspects of methodology. The first concern the allocation of roles in the classroom. A teacher has to 'perform' rather than 'to teach', *i.e.*, he or she must participate in activity with the pupils as an equal partner and not as the one who supplies 'correct behaviour'. The second major aspect of a communicative methodology is feedback. This has to be provided in such a way that learners can subconsciously test hypothesis about the target language. The 'input' will be determined by the natural process of adaptation and negotiation that all communicative enterprises generate. Traditional correction procedures, which we follow, has a limited value for acquisition. Instead of these, other devices—repetition, expansion, extensions, prompting and modelling are more useful. These are the natural tools of communication for maintaining the flow.

The traditional methodology, based on separate stages for presentation, mechanical practice and contextual practice, does not meet the requirements of a communicative methodology for acquisition. Thus in spite of materials being communicative, their value for acquisition is lost due to teacher's insistence on a pedagogic role and on rigorous formal correction procedure. Brumfit (1985) has argued that 'fluency' (which stem from acquired rather than learnt knowledge) can best be fostered by a methodology in which pupils first 'communicate as far as possible with all available resources', followed by presentation and drilling if a 'need' is demonstrated. Here what is said is always in the hands of the learner.

A teaching need, for a language work, demands to produce work for display to the teacher in order that evaluation and feedback could be supplied directly with the demand to perform adequately in the kind of natural circumstances. Language display for evaluation tended to lead to a concern for accuracy, monitoring, reference rules, possibly explicit knowledge, problem solving and evidence of skill getting. In contrast, language use requires fluency, expression rules, a reliance on implicit knowledge and automatic performance. On occasions, it requires monitoring and problem solving strategies, but these will not be the most important features.

Among teachers there is a misconception about teaching English. It is firmly believed that one must follow the grammatical rules and authenticity of a language should be measured on the basis of accuracy of the language display. However, for communicative purpose, fluency is no less important than formal accuracy (Brumfit 1984). The functional use of the language is fulfilled when one is able to communicate with other without significant pauses for an extended period. For developing this ability (fluency), monitoring must be unconscious or automatic, and the quality of the talk is less important than the quantity. The work displayed must have coherent, reasoned and "semantically dense" sentences, showing a "mastery of the semantic and syntactic resources of the language", so that the speaker does not become tongue tied with strangers or lost for words when an unexpected situation arises. He does very rapid pre-editing of what he says and he is quickly able to look over a large range of alternative ways of responding to a situation and chooses the one that sounds most sonorous or apt. We need not deny the value of accuracy in ELT, but it should be clear from the above discussion that it is not necessary for everyone and certainly is not sufficient for anyone. For functional use of language, less emphasis on accuracy is beneficial to the fluency of the SL learners. Therefore, fluency is to be regarded as natural language use, whether or not it results in native-speaker-like language comprehension or production. Then the question arises where does the difference lie? When observed closely, it is found that we miss or do not care for the following important aspects of such natural language use:

1. Language produce should have been produced by the speaker.
2. The content should be determined by the speaker or writer.
3. Normal process of adjustment to the demands of a changing situation will be necessary.
4. The objective of the activity should be quite distinct from the formation of appropriate or correct language.
5. Students should not be made to feel the intervention by the teacher as teacher rather than as communicator during the performance of the activity. But the crucial point is that the teacher's greater power to determine what is or is not appropriate behaviour should not affect students' freedom

to hide or reveal their own intimate feelings or personal information, in the same way as they would be free to choose in a non-pedagogic environment.

6. Correction should have either no place, or a very minor place, in fluency work, for it normally distracts from the message.

Brumfit (1984) in an interim model of the language teaching process tries to indicate how teacher's activities can affect the learning process of a learner. He says that in the process of formal, accuracy based teaching, together with specific correction by the teacher (of any aspect of language) will not necessarily have any immediate impact below the level of consciousness. Production for test purposes proceeds from learned abilities which may or may not have been assimilated to the underlying knowledge of the system of the language. Indeed, if testing follows too rapidly on teaching, it may well only test unassimilated language items. But during the process of a language use (after a considerable period of time), learner genuinely and spontaneously can either comprehend without effort or produce appropriately. Some lexical items may apparently become fully internalised almost at once. Many other items will be apparently useable only after months or may never appear to be comprehended, or more frequently produced. Heavy emphasis on fluency activities, the conversion of conscious knowledge to unconscious knowledge will be facilitated. This may be because reference rules are more or less conscious while expression rules are rules of association and creation of schemata. Accuracy activities aim at conscious learning by students, but the conversion of the tokens of the language into clue-laden system with genuine communicative potential requires fluency activities in which the learner's focus is on meaning rather than form.

In May 1982, Dr. Prabhu submitted a paper at the TESOL Convention, Honolulu, which is known as Bangalore Project. The basic assumption of the project is that 'term is best learnt when the learner's attention is on meaning (Prabhu 1982). This is based on the belief that the process of grammar construction by the learner is likely to be a developmental process which is 'organic' rather than 'additive'. We have no reason to assume that observer's generalisations about language structure correspond to those involved in learner's grammar construction; such observers' generalisations, being based on 'fully-formed' language competence, will frequently conflict with those that are part of an interlingual grammar; and consequently any conscious formulation of generalisations is likely to be harmful rather than beneficial as it will distort the learner's own generalisation by imposing inappropriate categories.

Evaluation and testing

Language testing is a form of study involving comparison of the proficiency of the same language (E.G. Lewis 1974). In testing second language achievement across nations and among different language group in the same nation, account has to be taken of the influence of the mother tongue and problems of positive and negative transfer. Ideally, a differential weightage, corresponding to the distance of the various mother tongues from the second language, is required. This in turn postulates some methods of linguistic level—phonology, grammar and semantics.

The teacher's need for information from tests is satisfied by a description of individual or group performance, or a prognosis or diagnosis of the difficulties a student may find himself faced within the learning a language.

Devies (1968) points out that language testing involves both linguistics and psychology because it is concerned with language and learning.

Earlier, language teaching was done by means of grammar-translation method, and what the student was expected to do was to translate into the second language expressions of any variety. No consideration was given to the needs of the learner. The associated linguistic theory is the traditionalist one, and since the learner is not taken into account, there is no theory of psychology involved. The needs of the learner are not considered except that some attempt is made to sequence the teaching material so that the beginner starts with the easiest material and progress to the more difficult as he becomes more fluent.

But there are some others who see language as a machine which acts as a stimulus-response mechanism. Therefore, teaching to them is to analyse language into its parts or, as it frequently said, structures. This term is used in isolation to refer to grammatical structures, ignoring the fact that other language levels, *e.g.*, phonology, semantics, have their structures too.

But those who hold a united view of language and language learning, view their process as creative and at the same time rule based. Language and language learning in their opinion are inter-dependent and there is no such thing in the world as a state of language separate from people and, therefore, from learning. The test must be much more situational because the teaching is.

In the discussion so far it is found that views on language teaching greatly affects the language testing system. Two basic modes of language teaching, which reflect itself in testing our learners at intermediate and undergraduate level, are presented. A typical intermediate test paper includes translation and rules of grammar, independent of other language features such as phonology, semantics, context etc. It is less concerned with 'pure' language features, e.g., segmental stress. What is more significant is that the language learner's creativity is being re-directed by allowing the learner to make use of the rules he has learnt in order to establish how far he has internalised them. This is very different from a multiple choice answer to a stimulus involving, say intonation, because what is being demanded is use of the rules to produce a sentence or response which is new. Therefore, it all depends on what the teacher is looking for.

Rebacca Valette (1977) brought out the second edition of her "Modern Language Testing" ten years after the first edition. This edition represents a considerable change in the views on language testing. Fig. 2.6 shows shift of emphasis in language testing:

It is clear from the Fig. 2.6 that in the language testing, the most useful kinds of tests are a combination of the two views, the analytical and the integrative. Test reliability is increased by adding to the stock of discrete items in a test. Validity, however, is increased by making the test truer to life.

Before going to evaluate an outline principles and techniques for specifying the communicative needs of language learners and assessing his language performance in terms of these needs, it is worthy to have a look on some basic linguistic principles and their application to testing:

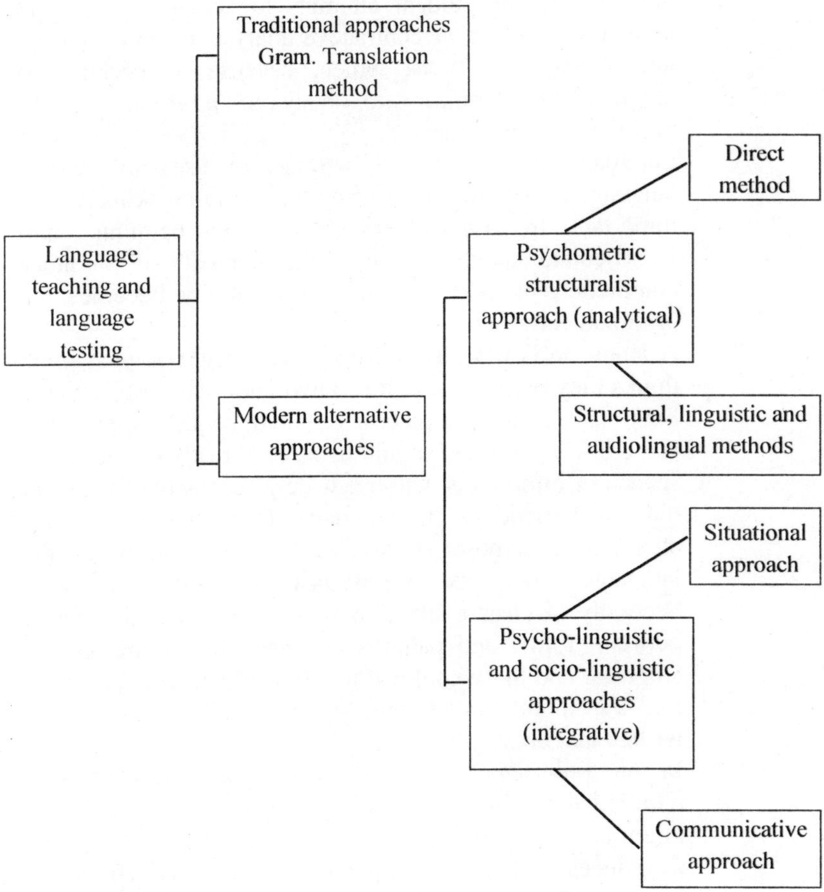

Fig. 2.6: Shift of Emphasis in Language Testing

1. Language is a set of habits in communication. A subject cannot truly be said to 'know a language', until he is able to respond quickly and automatically to natural language situations. The test writer must decide to what extent, if any speech should be a factor in this test. Another very important implication for the writer both of texts and language tests is that learning of a second language involves the learning of a second set of language habits, one can and must anticipate interference from the first

language as the student attempts to acquire the second language. The use of contrastive analysis to point out the new language patterns which, because of background language interference, are likely to pose the greater problems to the learner.

2. Language is speech, not writing. In tests of general language proficiency, measuring the aural/oral skills is fully important. In case of tests designed for beginning and intermediate students. The measurement of auditory comprehension and oral production ability becomes the prime objective.

3. A language is what its native speakers say, not what some thinks they ought to say. It has two important implications. First, that language materials should be descriptive, not prescriptive. *i.e.*, they should be based directly on the actual speech of informants who use widely acceptable social and regional varieties of the language. They should not make attempts to impose an artificial, 'ideal' variety of the language which has no existence outside the classroom. Secondly, a clear distinction must always be maintained between forms and patterns characteristic of the spoken language and those confined to, or clearly more appropriate for, the more formal and 'grammatically conservative' written language.

In the 'pre-scientific' era of language testing, most tests required the subjects to make a series of decisions about grammatical 'correctness'. Directions simply asked the examinees to choose or write the 'correct forms'. But in the best of today's tests of SLS, a careful distinction is made between problems involving the colloquial language and those calling for sensitivity to written style. Contexts are written to reflect colloquial usage, with other phenomena of the spoken language. Regarding tests we still stick to the pre-scientific era. Directions given on tests paper simply asked the examinees to choose or write the correct forms. The level of usage is seldom explicitly identified, and the context of the items often omitted if given, it ranged only to the literary contexts. A single example, taken from a widely used test of English for second language students is taken up for consideration.

Direction—Insert 'shall', or 'will' in the following:

Don't worry, I __________ have plenty of time".

Even our language materials are of prescriptive type. They are not based on actual but are of 'ideal' variety, which has no existence outside the classroom. They do not have a distinct idea between forms and patterns characteristics of the spoken language and to those confined to the more formal and 'grammatically conservative' written language.

4. Languages are different. Moulton (1961) says, "an attempt to describe those 'exotic' tongues with no grammatical relationship to European languages are futile attempts and attempting word for word translations is not possible, since the full meaning of a word in one language can rarely be matched by a word in another language and, therefore, no translation is ever fully satisfactory. The ability to translate elegantly is a special skill quite different from ability to speak, understand, read and write."

The actual manifestation of linguistic competence in behaviour is called linguistic performance and is affected by a large number of non-linguistic variables. It may happen that a learner/examinee might possess a perfectly adequate set of language habits and yet not be able or willing to speak on a given occasion. The person may have a temporary block whereby he forgets a certain word (Brown and McNeill, 1966) or the person to whom he is speaking may embarrass him to the stumbles and stutters in his speech. There will still inevitably be variation in the degree to which the speaker's utterances conform to his underlying competence; he may start a sentence and cut it off in midstream, produce a chance inaccurate pronunciation, or through inattention say a word he did not intend to say. Likewise, in hearing or reading language material, the individual's actual degree of comprehension on a particular occasion may not measure up to what he is capable of.

There are individual differences, both in competence and performance variables, that may be a function of either constitutional or experiential variables. Both kinds of variables have substantial weight in the determination of the individual's competence and ability in performance. The language tester has to develop procedures that will validly measure the degree of competence possessed by an individual, regardless of how he acquired it. Neither language competence nor language performance varies along a single dimension. It is not the case that an individual who have a degree of competence in one part of the vocabulary of a language will necessarily have corresponding competence in another part of the vocabulary nor will he necessarily have a comparable degree of competence in the syntax or the phonology of the language. But practically it would be impossible to attempt the assessment of each particular habit in a language. We can only sample from the array of possible habits.

Since learning a language makes much more use of written material than does learning a native language, competence in spoken and written aspects may develop somewhat independently, therefore, these competences must be separately assessed. It is useful to start from a classification of different areas of language competence in which individual differences are to be sought and measured (Davies, 1968). Linguistic performance varies with respect to the following dimensions:

(a) Speed of response,
(b) Diversity of response,
(c) Complexity of information processing, and
(d) Awareness.

These dimensions can apply differentially to various aspects of linguistic competence phonology, lexion and grammar. For a clear notion of the possible diversity of language testing tasks and of examining what kind of competences and performances they can measure. It is helpful to develop a classification scheme. We have the following Table 2.1 for testing purposes, so that the items actually appearing in the cells are test techniques.

A skill such as reading which we may now designate an 'old type' skill will appear in a number of different places in this table. It will appear under Receptive as Reading comprehension and under Productive as Reading aloud. Or, if preferred, both Reading comprehension and Reading Aloud could appear under the joint Receptive and Productive, though for different reasons. Reading aloud is an activity which necessarily involves both channels. Reading comprehension necessarily involves only comprehension. Production is introduced only in order to manifest to someone else that the comprehension has taken place. Reading is best regarded as number of skills, not as a single skill. Reading comprehension may, therefore, be a technique for eliciting control over the 'old type' skill of reading, reading itself, then through Reading Comprehension and other techniques may be better regarded as a means of approaching a more basic skill such as Semantics or Language organisation.

Table 2.1: Test Techniques

	Channels		
	Productive	Both (P&R)	Receptive
Extra Linguistic skills	Free Essay	Interview	
Semantic Skills	Oral composition Vocabulary Networks	Dictation Questions and Answers	Listening Comprehension Reading Comprehension
Organisational Skills	Reading Speed	Reading Aloud	Intonation (minimal pairs) Grammatical Sensitivity
Motor Perceptive Skills	Phoneme Approximations Stress		Phoneme Discrimination Stress

(Adapted from Davies 1968: 11).

Language testing is very much concerned with evaluation. There are two contrasting examination procedures. The first or 'subjective' procedure is that in which the examinee answers in his own words and at appropriate length, all or some of a relatively small number of questions. Typical key words in the question set in examination of this kind are 'Discuss' 'Compare', 'Contrast', 'Describe' and the answers they elicit may range from a single sentence to a dozen or more paragraphs. The whole examination is of the 'essay' type. Assessment of the examinee's work is 'subjective' in the sense that its merit has to be evaluated or judged by the examiner.

Two examples of 'essay type' questions requiring answers of very different length are:

(a) Discuss Shakespeare's Sonnets, and

(b) Who said the following, and to what end?
'The quality of mercy is not strained;
It droppeth as the gentle rain from Heaven
Upon the place beneath'.

The second or 'objective' procedure is that in which the examinee responds to each of a large number of questions by selecting one or more of several alternative answers provided with the question; by supplying a single word; or by some other process (reflecting the ingenuity of the compiler of the examination) indicating his knowledge or lack of knowledge of the pre-determined correct answer. Assessment of the merit of the examinee's work is 'objective' in the sense that no evaluative judgment is needed on the part of the examiner. A marking key, previously prepared, is all that is required and even this is redundant if the examination is compiled with machine marking or scoring in mind.

Two examples illustrating different types of objective items are:

(a) Some words are missing in the following lines of poetry, underline in the brackets the words that fits each space best.

Down on the hillside stood the trees,

1. Their song was self and . . . . . ;
(shrill/clear/sharp/low/sweet)
2. The blossoms in the gentle . . . . .;
(wind/breeze/trees/hands/glows)
3. Were . . . . . ; like the snow.
(falling/freezing/self/while/not) and

(b) In the sentences below underline the one word you would stress to make clear (without actually saying) what is in the brackets.

1. Please close your desk lids gently now (do not make a loud noise)
2. Please close your desk lids gently now (do it immediately).

(adapted from Davies 1968).

By the term 'subjected' we mean 'requiring judgment' and by 'objective we simply mean 'automatic'.

Requirements of Good Examination and Test Procedures

As with other tools, the efficacy of an examination or test cannot be gauged in isolation from the procedure of which it is a part, or the purpose to which it is a part. A test useful in one situation may be useless in another.

An examination or test, if it is to be efficient, must discriminate the subjects examined or tested both reliably and validly.

(i) *Discrimination:* The purpose of the instrument, whether examination or test, is to reflect differences in the attributes concerned which are presumed to exist among the subjects. In the field of language testing, the attribute may be the extent of vocabulary, ability to spell, power of comprehension, control of language in speech or writing or any other attribute considered sufficiently important to merit testing. The extent to which a single subject manifests the attribute becomes meaningful only in relation to the corresponding manifestations by others. An examination is to tell us something about an individual, it must be capable of discriminating among the group of which he is a member.

(ii) *Reliability*: Only discrimination is not enough for an examination, but it must be consistent in the discrimination it makes. Scores on it must be reliable *i.e.*, on repeating the procedure:
   (a) the score should not be subject to fluctuations and, hence,
   (b) the persons obtaining these scores should maintain their standings relative to one another.

There is no one reliability coefficient characterizing a test or examination (for detail please see Davies 1968). Depending upon the procedure used, no less than four different coefficient can be derived from testing or examining one group of subjects. Moreover, the scatter of ability in the group itself also affects the outcome. A well made objective test of English vocabulary designed for non-native speakers, is likely to show a high reliability coefficient, no matter which procedure is used. The same test, administered to native speakers, will probably show a lower co-efficient. The constructors of a language test should, therefore, report

(a) the procedure used in estimating reliability, and
(b) the nature of the group used in its estimation.

It is well known that the marks, awarded by different markers or even by the same marker on different occasions, are frequently inconsistent with each other when the process of assessment demands subjective judgement. From the statistical point of view, there are three main causes of disagreement among markers who independently mark the same set of scripts:

(a) The marks awarded may differ in average standard or level. One marker may be generally severe, another generally lenient.
(b) The marks may differ in their scatter or spread. One marker may employ the whole range of the available scale, another only part of it.
(c) The marks may order the examinees differently. Discrepancies among the markers in rank order are reflected in low inter-correlations among the arrays of the marks awarded.

To overcome or reduce the marker unreliability and to improve the consistency of subjective judgments with the marking of essays three measures are used:

(1) Analytical procedures: Marking control is sought by the isolation and separate assessment of different aspects of the material to be marked. Each aspect is allocated a mark

out of same maximum which reflects a previously made judgement of its importance in relation to the whole. Which particular aspect should be isolated obviously depends on the purpose of the examination. One analytic scheme, suggested for marking in essay included in an examination of English as SL, is as follows:

(a) Content

(b) Formal structure of the essay as a whole

(c) Language:

- (i) Sentence structure
- (ii) Morphology
- (iii) Spelling
- (iv) Punctuation
- (v) Richness of vocabulary

(d) Misinterpretation of the subject.

(adapted from Davies, 1968)

Studies made by Cast (1939) strongly suggest that the assessment made by a single marker who uses a framework of this sort are more reliable than 'global' impression assessment made by one person.

(2) Increasing the number of questions.

(3) Increasing the number of examiners.

(iii) *Validity*—Validity of any examination or test procedure may be broadly defined as the extent to which it does what it is intended to do (If validity is to be achieved, discrimination and reliability are necessary conditions. But they are not sufficient). A test may discriminate well and performance on it may be capable of reliable assessment, but it is invalid if it fails to test what it should. Whenever we find bad agreement between different measurements, then we can safely say that the examination is bad. We can produce following scheme for validation:

Pilliner (1952) deals with the meaning of validity and its implications in evaluation. He discusses three major kinds of validity: predictive, concurrent and content.

Table 2.2: Scheme for Validation

Type	*Related to*	*Criterion*
Face	⟶	Lay view of language
Content	⟶	Syllabus analysis
Construct	⟶	Theory of aims in Language Teaching
Predictive	⟶	Later test of language ability
Concurrent	⟶	Another test or measure (*e.g.*, teacher's assessment) of language ability given at same time

Predictive validity is a quantitative concept. The Davies English Proficiency Test is designed to select for control of English among non-native English speakers who intend to study in Britain. Its predictive validity will be measured by its success in selecting those students whose proficiency in English is adequate for the courses they intend to take and the criterion will be the assessments of that proficiency made by their teacher in Britain.

But examinations and tests have another purpose, besides prediction of later success. It is axiomatic that their content inevitably influences the teaching and learning which precede them. However, the influence of the examination or test is not necessarily bad. Properly constructed, it can foster and reinforce good teaching and sound learning. To achieve these ends, the test constructor must start with a clear conception of the aims and purposes of the area of learning to which his test is relevant. If the content of his test directs the previous learning of potential testees towards the achievement of these aims and purposes; and if that content enables the test user to evaluate the extent to which the testees have achieved these aims; then the test possesses content validity. Wiseman (1961) says : "The syllabus content approach tends to perpetuate ineffective educational practices; it is a reactionary instrument helping to encapsulate method within the shell of tradition and accepted practice". But "the goal-oriented test is exactly the opposite; it evaluates learning and teaching in terms of the aims of the curriculum, and so fosters critical awareness, good method and functional content". If the aim of the teaching English is specific as fluency in speech and literacy in reading and writing, then the English examination should be directed at testing this fluency and literacy. There is no need to include in the examination questions on the terminology of formal grammar, even though some teachers consider it a powerful tool in developing literacy in their pupils and, hence, include it in their syllabus. That means the syllabus is a means to an end, and should be regarded as such. It is essential that these aims be specified in concrete and not abstract terms. Thus, content validity is concerned with the relationship between test or examination content and detailed curricular aim.

(iv) *Items from English Language Tests*
  I. Grammatical structures
  II. Listening test
  III. Reading comprehension
  IV. Word order of a sentence
(v) *Essay Subjects*
  For detail study, please see Davies (1968)

Earlier, as we have seen, assessment must be made for communicative performance in concrete terms of abilities, skills or attitudes. The key role played by the specification of communicative needs in the development of language curricula and the derivation of the design of both language programmes testing systems. It can be illustrated by the curriculum triangle (Carroll 1980).

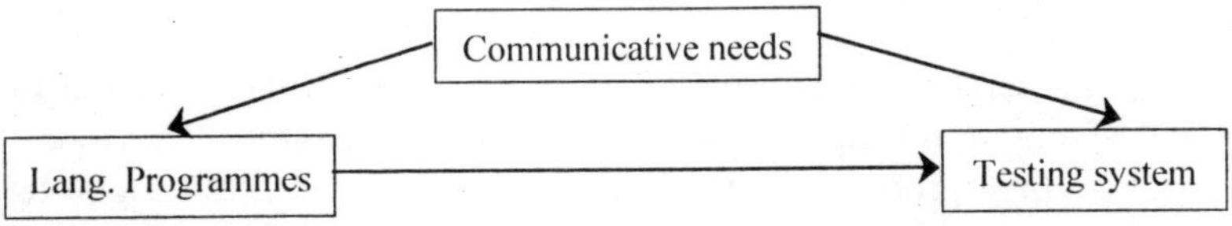

This diagram illustrates the interactive relationship between the language programme and the testing system and their natural derivation from an analysis of the learner's communicative needs. The development of tests for assessing communicative performance has been greatly influenced by current ideas about the role of language communication and, in particular, by the implication of those ideas for the teaching and testing of language for specific purposes. Approaches to problems of language testing are strongly influenced by the place accorded to usage and use in inter-personal communication. The ultimate criterion of language mastery is, therefore, the learner's effectiveness in communication for the settings he find himself in. Therefore, distinction between usage and use is of great importance for teaching and testing. A test cannot be based on selection of items chosen on linguistic grounds alone, and to devise an effective test, it is necessary to specify how a testee requires to use the language. The criterion for success lies not in formal correctness but in communicative effectiveness. There are rules of use without which the rules of grammar would be useless. Our selection of items emphasises the usage point of view in which language is seen as a unified entity with fixed grammatical patterns and a core of commonly-used lexical items. Equipped with the mastery of these language patterns, it is hoped, our learners should learn to cope with the situations they find themselves in. But different patterns of communication will entail different configurations of language skill mastery and, therefore, a different course of test content. From "the use" point of view, language loses its appearances of unity and must be taught and tested according to the specific needs of the learner. In our classes there are learners with heterogeneous needs so our courses are of general kind and have no specific objectives.

The adaptation of the criteria of communicative use presents many difficulties to the tester. So diversified testing based on usage is in vogue here.

Issues in Communicative Testing

There are certain issues, says Carroll (1981), particularly related to the devising of instruments for measuring communicative behaviour.

The first problem is to discover how to carry out rigorous measurement of language-based performance and yet keep intact the essential features of communicative behaviour. There are two solutions to this problem:

(a) To pick out particular language features, (especially those likely to cause difficulties, present them one after the other in a test and assess the testee's general proficiency from the number to which he gives a 'correct' response. But it is more likely that these easily devised objectively scored tests of strings of linguistics items may miss the essence of the measurement of communicative performances. Detaching test items, forming their communicative context, are to risk finding little about the learner's behaviour. Actually this thing has happened here.

(b) The other solution to the isolated or discrete approach to items writing is the 'cloze test'. But this is still essentially usage based. The task does not represent genuine interactive communication and is, therefore, only an indirect index of potential efficiency in coping with day-to-day communicative tasks.

Another focus of discussion has been the distinction between norm-referenced and criterion-referenced test, *i.e.*, between comparing the performance of individual with that of other individuals in a sample of comparable persons, as against comparing his performance with pre-determined behavioural criteria.

In measuring human behaviour, especially in its more complex field such as language, the issues are not so clear-cut. The classical measurement framework has been to assess performance not by direct reference to criterion, but by a comparison of the performance of an individual with that of others on the same measure, expressing his competence in terms of group norms and predicting the likelihood of his success in a task.

Certain curricular areas, such as Mathematics, Science and Sports are more amenable to criterion referenced approach. Here the task, experiments, calculation can be clearly specified and the result can be judged more easily as regards success and failure. But in language teaching, however, the targets and criteria have been so nebulous and indeterminate that performance have had to be assessed in terms of norms.

In the performance priority is given, as Carroll (1980) says, to descriptions of actual communicative behaviour such as, 'can handle interjections', 'responds to tones' etc. They have to clarify the level of performance of such behaviour in specifically linguistic or usage features such as, 'can interpret accurately lexical and grammatical usage and the significance of variations in tone and stress patterns'. In other words, our criteria are communicative behavioural features which subsume the linguistically based skills used for performing the task.

In the performance rating sheet the three categories of 'vocabulary', 'grammar' and 'pronunciation' are included. But such categories are essentially those of language-based usage; they refer not to the final criteria of communicative performance but to contributory and subordinate 'enabling' skills related to, but not identical with, communicative skills. One communicative activity or function can be realised in a number of language patterns (for detail please see Davies 1968: Chap. 1). These responses may allow the testee to achieve his communicative purpose but it is impossible to predict which one will be used. The adequacy of his response will depend both on the extent of his linguistic resources and on his skill in deploying them; on whether he uses a limited stock. It is the use of the language that ultimately decides the user's effectiveness in handling communicative situations. That is why, our learners remain unable to communicate in it despite having spent seven years in learning the subject/language.

The third issue of 'authenticity' is an important aspect of any discussion on language testing. All tasks undertaken should be real-life, interactive communicative operations and not the typical routine examination response to the tester's 'stimuli', or part of a stimulus-response relationship; that the language of the test should be day-to-day discourse, not edited or doctored in the interests of simplification but presented with all its expected irregularities, that the contexts of the interchanges are realistic, with the ordinary interruptions, background noises, and irrelevancies found in the airport or lecture room; and that the rating of a performance, based on its effectiveness and adequacy as a communicative response, will rely on non-verbal as well as verbal criteria.

It is obvious how different from these are many of our language tests. What language stimulus it provides is a multiple choice item of language structure such as:

He eats meat ____________ (a) doesn't he?
(b) won't I?
(c) can't you?

Even these test tasks which require the use of real, live language usually do so in a very artificial setting—'describe in 100 words how a bicycle works'—an unreal assignment, which few people would undertake in ordinary life. Or let us consider the tasks lying midway between the closed multiple choice items and the open ended writing such as a cloze test; in which one is asked to replace word. It is claimed that this is a test of basic linguistic processing mechanism, of grammar, of prediction, but it is not a credible communicative task. These conventional tests ignore certain features of genuine language use, which are that language is interactive, unpredictable, purposive, authentic, contextualised, based in performance and assessed in terms of behavioural outcomes. It is true at present we are not testing genuine communicative performance at all, but artificial, language like behaviour.

However, 'authenticity' in itself cannot provide the total answer to the testing power. Hence test tasks must be drawn from a range of inter-related systems, from consciously systematised functions, skills and linguistic categories, brought together in the performance of an authentic communicative operation, performance whose value is judged by reference to the satisfactory resolution of patterns of communication, function, skill and language measurements.

A good test will show an optimum balance of four characteristics:

(a) Relevance,
(b) Acceptability,
(c) Comparability, and
(d) Economy.

It becomes obvious that these tests do not reflect the specifications identified in an analysis of common needs, at the same time the test information did not guide decisions about the teacher's performance to the greater extent. This puts a question mark on the relevance of the tests. Occasionally, our learners did not accept its content and format.

Various processes required to make specification of test content are shown in Table 2.3:

After a look at this communicative competence specification Table, it is found that upto what mark consider it for specification of test content, we design to specify test contents from the course designer's viewpoint. We have to identify our participants by giving relevant information about his identity and language background, such as his age, sex, nationality, place of residence as well as his mother tongue. Though earlier it was not accorded any importance in construction of a course or test. But now these play an important role.

Table 2.3: Communicative Competence Specification

	Identification of participant(s)		
Communicative needs Processor	Purpose →	Setting →	Interaction Instrumentality
	↓	↓	↓
	Dialect	Target level	Event/activity Key
Skills/functions selector	Language skills		Units of meaning (functions and tones)
Specification	Syllabus content and/or Test content		

(adapted from Carroll (1980))

The current emphasis is on socio-linguistic features of communication. The activities specified are processed into communicative functions, which accompanied by their appropriate attitudinal tone markers are called 'units or meaning'. Psycho-social and social relationship plays an important role in units of meaning.

We find after a look at the communicative competence (need) specification that our test papers do not usually have a clear view of the learners' need and its translation into its further macro and micro units. Our test items are of traditional type. It is repeated again and again with only minor changes which we have discussed above. In testing communicative performance one thing is often forgotten, that is about the mode use for test. Usually, we think the isolated modes – writing, speaking and listening must be tested in isolation. But isolated modes seem to represent rather unrealistic tasks and testing them in isolation takes us away from reality. It can be said that mixed mode test is 'impure' and that we will not know precisely which mode we are testing (Davies 1968: Chapter 2). There are tests such as listening, reading and writing (the imaginative essay or the description of a picture, enacted or remembered event) which can be tested by single-focus (mode) tests, but speaking cannot be. In practice, speech is part of an interactive chain and it is unreal to expect to be able to test it as an isolated language activity. It depends upon other modes to test it.

Evaluation is last step to testing procedures, says Heuri Holee, (1980). It determines how far the result aimed at, corresponds with the result achieved and which, therefore, checks that the objectives have been reached. It implies that there are performances to be judged, critical criteria and levels of reference should be determined. The learner produces performances which are 'relevant' or susceptible to the check in all the activities in which he participates, whether expression, comprehension or even metalinguistic, going from drills including each separate items—to interactions with native speakers or work on authentic documents. The learner has to take part in real acts of communication, since this is the only way in which the match between results achieved and results aimed at can be confirmed. Examples of the sort of occasion where this is possible includes:

(a) interaction with native speakers;
(b) listening comprehension with authentic recording; and
(c) reading documents produced for 'real' reading *e.g.*, letters which will really be 'posted' abstracts or articles which will be published and so on.

But our tests do not evaluate these aspects. There is no question of interaction with native speakers. The other two also have no place in our tests. Every evaluation of a performance is carried out on the basis of specific criteria or specific combination of criteria. Not all examiners necessarily use the same criteria or the same combinations of criteria, nor do they regard the same criteria as equally important. This reflects their choice of importance and the sort of skill they want to have of that particular test.

Examiners generally evaluate in terms of levels. Either they opt for nine band system or grading system. But most of our college examinations evaluate the examinees in terms of marks accorded for the particular item. The levels of achievements which are chosen vary according to what aspect of performance is being evaluated and are directly related to the relative degree of importance accorded to the aspect in question. These levels vary from examiner to examiner.

The need to make judgements on errors derives from two

sources:

(a) The need to assess a learner's knowledge for administrative purposes (the assignment of grades/marks); and
(b) to determine priorities for remedial measures.

R. Alexander (1988) points out there is a complex relationship between course, the language proficiency and examination requirements. So we might apply a crude three-fold analysis of what is involved in an oral examination:

Oral Examination

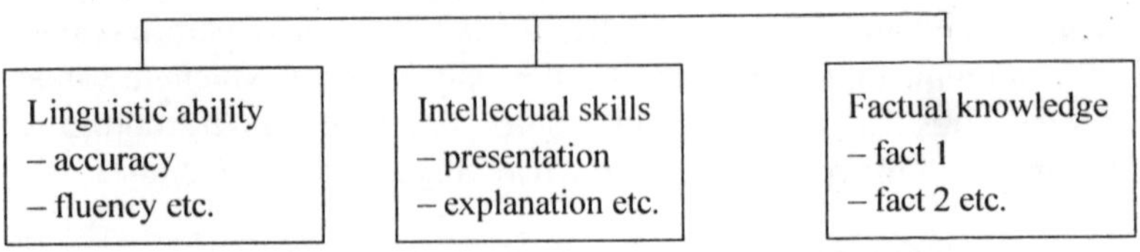

It is clear from this array of factors that testing/examining of oral proficiency will become progressively more difficult as the level of proficiency increases. Any assessment of the production of the testee/ examinee will have to depend on considerations of communicative success and/or intelligibility, as Perren (1968) puts:

> "Intelligibility is not merely the production of identifiable sounds in a conventional order; it depends on a situation which includes a particular listener. The meaning of what is said must be the final criterion and it can only be judged by reference to a context of situations and audience."

The focus on oral proficiency, as had already been stated, stems from the principled assumption that ability to talk face to face in the second language is perhaps the crucial ability to be sampled for the purposes of the examination procedure laid down by the regulations.

Our syllabus is grossly divided into skills and content. There are further subdivisions of its components but it is not done in terms of micro-functions. In some schools whole score is evaluated by giving weightage for periodic tests, semester tests and annual tests. But such marking is not done at college level. Examination is not concerned with the students' functional skill in English; what is tested is their ability to memorise the contents of the text books. Hence, marks obtained do not show their proficiency in the skill acquired on the language but their capacity to memorise the contents of the text books. The weightage given to each aspect of the language is as follows:

Paper I

Prose (describing)	30 per cent
Poetry (Summary)	10 per cent
Poetry (comprehension)	14 per cent
Play (Character sketch or summary)	15 per cent
Story (Character sketch or summary)	15 per cent
Sentence framing (words given)	8 per cent
Matching words (meaning)	8 per cent

Paper II

Essay/Composition	14 per cent
Letter writing	10 per cent
Paragraph writing	10 per cent
Comprehension	12 per cent
Translation	10 per cent
Grammatical items	44 per cent

It is obvious that our evaluation system demands descriptive language, which is very rarely used in day-to-day work. Other functional items have no place in the evaluation system.

Socio-cultural Variables

Society and its culture are the contexts in which a person lives, thinks and feels. It is the identity of which each of us is an integral part. Kundu (1982) describes culture as a force which guides the life style of people.

A language grows in the culture and bears the imprint of the culture. Therefore, language teaching and learning situation is greatly influenced by the socio-cultural factors. This variable is discussed in detail in Chapter 3.

Guardian, Society and Non-linguistic Factors

The interaction of environment mechanism and resultant situation is responsible for actual language use in society. Assumptions, belief, customs all play an important role in building up the mind set of a learner. The environment is the sum total of the socio-cultural setting of the learner, says S.K. Sawhney (1990), of which his family, peer group, school and college and other people around him in the society are important components. Thoughts and belief of a person are moulded by the environment of the society in which he lives. That is why, ELT situation in this vast country of ours, with its tremendous diversity in environments and cultures, presents a highly complex picture. Darbhanga, though a city, has a mixed type of environment. One can call it half rural and half urban. Maithili is the dominant language and its speakers have distinctive socio-cultural feature. All these features are reflected in their response to ELT. Due to exposure to the mass-media and educational explosion, attitudinal changes are taking place. Earlier education of children was not considered as important as the acquisition of landed property. The change is most pronounced in the sudden growth of female education. People of lower strata are also keen to send their wards to public schools.

A child's verbal behaviour reflects his family background. Le Page (1968) states that the community within which the individual interacts with different groups with a shared language variety is the individual's speech community. The nature and the extent of the individual's interaction may differ from group to group. This fact is obvious from the economic background of the learner. Nida (1956) and Spolsky (1969) feel that the learner's attitude to a language affects the nature and intensity of his motivation to learn that language. Lambert (1967) and Nida (1956) consider attitude itself to be a cultural factor. Thus, an individual's verbal system is likely to resemble that of any other(s) only to the extent that the individual is motivated to do so.

In spite of their present positive attitude to English, the learning-teaching situation of English has not improved. There are many reasons for it. First of all, since guardians/parents themselves are not so literate that they can help their children. If some are literate they do not have enough time to help their children. If they find their wards score good marks in examination they become satisfied and never try to see their progress. This attitude makes students mistake their goal to be the scores, by foul means or fair, in the examination without bothering to cultivate language skills.

Among the non-linguistic factors are the growing frequency of strikes and bundh that disrupts the teaching programmes. Another problem is that of holding examinations of other classes. During that period, most of the classes are dropped or their durations shortened.

College environment also affects learning/teaching situation. It depends upon the attitude shown by the college authority. If a college has favourable climate, both for its staff and students, it is reflected in the performance profile of the students. But on the contrary, those colleges which have not built up an interactive infrastructure and cling to the old colonial methods of teaching are gradually losing their importance as teaching centres.

The academic anarchy prevailing in the state is reflected in the thorough dislocation of academic calendar and disruption of the session. In some universities the pending backlog of examination is being cleared on 'war-footing' level totally overlooking the necessity of attendance/learners in the class or the need for completing the prescribed syllabus for a particular course before allowing the students to sit for the examination. Model questions are being provided by the university as compensation for loss of reading hours along with other 'privileges' which are not conducive to the conduct of fair examination. This may appear to be a dismal scene indicating the total collapse of the old model of syllabus and classroom teaching. However, one significant fact has emerged from the chaos. The examination is now totally delinked from learning because it does not reflect in any way a reliable form of evaluation. While a large number of students now are approaching the task of learning English for acquiring the skills of the language use, they are not at all concerned with their university examinations for which model questions and answers are freely available. A new awareness is gradually gathering force, they now approach the teachers to learn the language and not for helping them to pass the examination for which they can fend for themselves. It is the time for the teacher to take advantage of the situation and to make the teaching/learning a meaningful exercise for both the learners and the teachers.

3

Socio-Cultural Aspects of ELT

Theories of Nativisation and its Function

Introduction

In India, Indian English is generally used as a second language, which is acquired after one has learnt a first language, or what is usually called the mother tongue. Kachru (1983) thinks that this results in interference or transfer from one's mother tongue in the second language. The problem of interference in Indian English becomes more complex, since the interference is caused by a large number of mother tongues. The Indian constitution recognises fifteen major languages, and the Census Report identifies over 1,652 languages and dialects.

The distinct socio-cultural parameters, in which English has been used in India, have resulted in a large number of innovations which have been termed Indianism (Kachru 1965). In this chapter we narrow down Indian English to Maithili English—a sub-variety of Indian English and consider linguistic interference and Maithili cultural context which makes it different from the general Indian English. Though it is not a fully developed dialectal form, its use by speakers of Mithila represents the basic trends of nativisation of English in India.

The variation in Indian English may be explained basically on three parameters: region, ethnic group and proficiency. Regional or geographical variation by and large coincides with the regional language such as Gujarati English (Harry 1962), Marathi English (Kelkar 1957), Tamil English (Gopalkrishnan 1960), Oriya English (T.K. Pramanik 1988), Hyderabadi English (S.V. Prasher 1979), Maithili English (Y.P. Yadav 1983; S.C. Chaudhary 1984), etc. are the mother tongues of the speakers of each variety. The ethnic variations cut across the regional language or dialect boundaries. The variations based on proficiency is crucial in the case of a second language. It ranges from educated Indian English to varieties such as Babu English, Butler English, Bearer English and Kitchen English (B.B. Kachru, 1983).

The consequence of this global use of English by non-native speakers has been that it is used in new social and cultural contexts and in contact with other languages. English is often 'nativised' (Kachru 1981b). That is, in each non-native context of use, new forms and functions of English develop, which are systematic and productive in that locale but which would be considered deviant in countries where English is spoken as a native language. The aggregate of these changes in a particular socio-linguistic setting delineates linguistically the non-native variety of that setting, in contrast with the established native speaker varieties, such as American, Canadian, British, Australian or New Zealand English.

Divergences from native speaker varieties result not from communicative strategies but from 'five main process of simplification' posited as universal in all second language acquisition by proponents of Error Analysis: "over generalisation, omission, reduction, substitution and restructuring" (Wong 1983).

The study of speech communities offers a large number of points of departure. Domains of language use have been described as the occasions on which one language (variant, dialect, style etc.) is habitually employed rather than another (Fishman 1966). Recurrent domains would be such as 'the family', 'the neighbourhood', 'governmental administration', 'occupation' and so forth. Other sources of variance are written/spoken medium, formal/informal styles, production/reception/inner speech etc. each insertion marked for choice and directions of change in choice of language. Some domains will be shown to be more and some less, maintenance prone in the given language-contact setting than others. The specific question of 'domains' is treated under the heading of 'functions' (Weinreich's *Language in Contact* 1953). In connection with 'language shifts', it is stated that these should be analysed in terms of the functions of the languages in the contact situations, since a mother tongue group may switch to new language in certain functions but not in other (Pride 1971).

In contexts where English is used daily as an international second language, these non-native varieties, or non-native English differ systematically from the native speaker varieties at almost all linguistic levels—phonology, morphology, syntax, semantics, style and discourse. In settings where the uses of English are generally in international functions, many of these differences from native varieties have generally been referred to by linguists as "ESL" (English as a second language) and "EFL" (English as foreign language) respectively. Kachru (1982b) considers ESL to be institutionalised varieties and EFL to be performance varieties. More area-centred research into non-native varieties to date has focused on institutionalised or performance varieties. Studies of performance varieties for India have been done by:

Das 1982;
Kachru 1965, 1966, 1973, 1976, 1978, 1983b;
Mehrotra 1982; and
Verma 1982.

Basic Socio-linguistic Concept

In order to clarify the approach some basic concepts in socio-linguistic deserve special elaboration or partial reinterpretation. The main concepts are:

Speech Community and Speech Fellowship

Hymes (1972) defines a speech community as a "community sharing rules for the conduct and interpretation of speech and rules for the interpretation of at least one linguistic variety. To this Gumperz (1972) adds "members of a speech community need not all speak the same language nor use the same linguistic forms on similar occasions. All that is required is that there should be at least one language in common and that rules governing basic communicative strategies be shared.

In that sense Mithila can be considered a speech community since the different groups of people of Darbhanga share the languages commonly used by different speech communities, namely, Hindi, Maithili, Urdu are variations of the powerful North Indian dialect. Maithili, however, enjoys the status of the main regional language as the largest number of people use this language for every day communication.

Firth's division of wide speech communities into smaller speech fellowships is a more useful level of analysis. A speech fellowship is that which shares not only a linguistic code but also a common context of culture and context of situation (Kachru 1981c). The context of culture comprises the entire linguistic and non-linguistic setting of speech fellowship, including social, cultural, political and economic variables. The context of situation consists of these aspects of the contexts of culture that are relevant to the actual use of language by members of a speech fellowship. The context of situation includes the following elements from the context of culture:

(a) The relevant features of participants: persons, personalities
  (i) Verbal actions of participants
  (ii) Non-verbal actions of participants
(b) The relevance of objects
(c) The effect of the verbal action

The other features to be considered are:

(a) Economic, religious and social structures to which participants belong;
(b) Type of discourse – monologue, narrative;
(c) Personal interchanges – age, sex of participants; and
(d) Types of speech – social flattery, cursing.

Within the socio-linguistic area of Mithila, the contexts of culture have distinct contexts of situation for the use of English. This study will analyse and compare the linguistic forms and functions of English as spoken and written by the speech fellowship of Mithila. A major goal of this study is to ascertain how a socio-linguistic area has resulted in identifiable patterns of change in the use and usage of English as an additional language.

Linguistic Repertoire

The goal of "socially realistic" linguistics (Kachru 1981c) is basically to describe and explain the forms and functions of language in the light of their inherent variation and the relationship of this variation to contexts of language use. This variation results from choices made from what Gumperz (1972) calls a speech community's "linguistic repertoire". Kachru (1982a) defines this linguistic repertoire as "the total range of codes which members of a speech community (or fellowship) have available for their linguistic interaction". Hymes (1984) says of this concept:

> "No normal human being talks the same way all the time. The daily experience of many millions of people includes a variety of languages or dialects. A variety of registers or styles is used and encountered. The abilities of individuals and the composite abilities of communities cannot be understood except by making 'verbal repertoire', not ' language', the central scientific notion".

The codes comprising a linguistic repertoire may be from distinct language families or dialects or styles of a single language (Kachru 1982a). It is apparent from Kachru's observation that in multilingual speech fellowship, such as Darbhanga, where variations occur at all these levels, the linguistic repertoire is more complex than in predominantly monolingual speech fellowship. Each language used by a multilingual speech fellowship, by virtue of its repeated contact with other languages, will diverge in many of its forms and functions from the same language used in a speech fellowship having a different linguistic repertoire.

Range and Depth

As a function of its context of culture and situation, each code in the linguistic repertoire of a given speech fellowship has a particular range of domains in which it is commonly used (*e.g.*, government, education, commerce, religion, family) and a depth of societal levels in the fellowship of people, who generally use it in these domains (*e.g.*, urban and rural; upper, middle and lower classes). In Mithila English is almost never the dominant code of discourse for any speaker in the domain of intra-national communication. Its use is generally restricted to the very few urban elites' code mixing of English (in certain domains) in their discourse. The extensive borrowing of English lexical items into Maithili is adopted by a large portion of the urban middle class and some of the working classes people.

Communicative Competence

For each code in the linguistic repertoire of a speech fellowship, members of the fellowship using the code share certain norms for its use and usage. These include norms of acceptability for formal features and norms of interpretation and appropriateness for the use of these specific communicative functions within the context of situation of the fellowship. The norms of interpretation and appropriateness are provided by the underlying shared culture; if the cultural norms are not shared or understood, the meaning of a text cannot be interpreted and its appropriateness cannot be determined. The degree to which a member of fellowship knows and can follow these norms for the codes used by the fellowship constitutes the member's communicative competence in the linguistic repertoire of the fellowship.

This definition has two important indications:

(a) Communicative competence in any linguistic code, including English, is not universal. Rather it is determined uniquely by the context of situation, including other languages with which that code is used.

(b) The various codes in the linguistic repertoire of a speech fellowship are not in free variation. Rather, selection of a given code, and its subsequent code switching and code mixing with other codes, are governed by complex context, specific rules of appropriateness related to its range and depth, including domain of language use, topic, mode and relative status of interlocutors and non-participant observers in a linguistic interaction. Knowledge of and ability to use each code appropriately in specific socio-linguistic contexts are included in communicative competence.

Deviations, Errors and Mistakes

Deviations can be distinguished from other divergences from the native speaker varieties by several criteria. Deviations are systematic, productive and stable in that they are shared by a large segment of a speech fellowship over an extended period of time. These deviations are functional in their contexts of situation, often with particular uses in specific domains.

Mistakes are occasional lapses in performance by native and non-native speaker of English from the norms of all varieties of English, they are not systematic, productive, stable or functional.

Errors in the acquisition of English by both native and non-native speakers are temporarily systematic, productive and functional. However, they are often idiosyncratic to individuals, and are not shared as acceptable and appropriate norms by the majority of the speech fellowship in which they are being used. Errors and mistakes are clearly markers of acquisitional and performance deficiencies; deviations, however, are not deficiencies.

Position of English in the Post-Colonial Era

The post-colonial era in India has witnessed considerable diversification in contexts of situation, resulting in additional differences in the spread and use of English in different regions. Our country is a socio-linguistic paradise. This has its rewards as well as disappointments. As R.P. Bhatnagar (1976) observes that one single cause of our dismal educational failure is our refusal to let millions of disadvantaged students use their own language for their education. We criminally overlook the colossal psychological harm we are doing to these disadvantage millions by imposing on them both a language and a language style not their own and thereby violating their personal and psychic identity. They will continue to be disadvantaged not because they are linguistically deprived or cognitively deficient, but because our educational system sets norms impossible for achievement except by a negligible minority of students belonging to the privileged class and constituting a favoured elite.

During the last few decades, however, the standard of English in India has deteriorated precipitously. The report of "The English Review Committee (1965)" reported by Bajpai : Pathak (1965) is true even today:

> "For weeks, even months, the students do not understand what his teachers say, he is unable to make notes; he cannot even take down correctly what is dictated; he cannot express himself correctly, in fact, what he writes makes no sense......His self-confidence is shattered and he develops an inferiority complex."

Prator's (1968) View is "Their English is characterised by 'bookish associations' and operates in a 'narrowly restricted range of situations', fulfilling only limited needs of communication". English is taught here as L_2 and one's mother-tongue habits are likely to stand in one's way. The paucity of resources, the scarcity of efficient and trained teachers in our schools and student's own lack of interest are largely responsible for this decline". Spolsky (1969) has also affirmed the significance of attitudes in the degree of proficiency one achieves in L_2 learning. Gardner and Lambert (1972) and Jakobovits (1970) have pointed out direct correlations between the learner's attitude, motivation and achievement. The linguistic skill in L_2, extending to the point of bilingualism, largely depends on the attitude of the family towards the members of the other ethnolinguistic group.

Parasher (1979a and 1979b) shows that English bilingualism in India became more widespread during the post-independence era. For Indian bilinguals English and mother tongue have well-defined functions. It becomes clear from Table 3.1:

Table 3.1: English Bilingualism

Sl. No.	*Domain*	*Speech*	*Writing*
1.	Family	Mainly MT/FL, Some ENGL	Mainly MT/FL, Some ENGL
2.	Friendship	ENGL and MT/FL	Mainly ENGL
3.	Neighbourhood	MT/FL and ENGL	
4.	Transactions	Mainly MT/FL and ENGL, Some Hindi or Reg.	
5.	Education	Mainly ENGL	ENGL
6.	Government	Mainly ENGL Some MT/FL	ENGL
7.	Employment	ENGL, a little MT/FL	ENGL

Note: MT = Mother tongue, FL = First language (Prasher 1979b)
REGL = Regional language, ENGL = English language.

The result shows that there is a strong agreement between the subject's language use and language performance. The picture that emerges is that the mother tongue is dominant in the family and friendship domain; English is dominant in the domain of education, government and employment and no language is dominant in the domains of neighbourhood and transactions.

The fact that language preferences are tilted in favour of English is a demonstration of the subjects' positive attitudes towards the language. Subjects' reporting English in the transaction domains indicates that they have strong positive attitudes towards English. One of the several factors responsible for the continued use of English in India seems to be positive attitudes of the elite towards English. As regards general reading (reading of magazines, papers), reading for work and reading to pleasure shows the following results:

Table 3.2: Language Preferences

Sl. No.	*Functions*	*English first preference*	*MT first preference*
1.	Reading newspapers	97.1 per cent	2.5 per cent
2.	Reading magazines	88.9 per cent	11.1 per cent
3.	Listening to broadcasts	21.2 per cent	72.0 per cent
4.	Reading for work	85.5 per cent	15.4 per cent
5.	Reading for pleasure	24.7 per cent	75.1 per cent

(Compiled by the author)

The Table 3.2 shows one reason why books and journals are read exclusively in English and specialised reading material is hard to find in the bilinguals' mother tongue. This is the reason why more bilinguals prefer to read newspapers and magazines in English may be because English newspapers and periodicals have a wider coverage as compared to those in Indian languages. But preference to mother tongue for reading for pleasure and listening to broadcasts show just an ambivalence of attitudes towards English.

Their preference for language of instruction in schools and universities as recorded in Table 3.3 shows that majority of the subjects think English to be the most suited medium of education beyond the primary level. Such a strong bias in favour of English as the most suited medium of education is based on the assumptions that it:

(a) helps in keeping the standards of education uniform throughout India;

(b) makes recent knowledge available to students;
(c) brightens the student's prospects of getting well-paid jobs in the country and abroad;

Table 3.3: Level of Education

Sl. No.	*Level of education*	*ENGL*	*MT/FL*	*Bilingual*
1.	Primary	29.2	48.7	21.2
2.	Secondary	52.1	11.7	35.8
3.	Undergraduate	85.1	2.5	11.9
4.	Postgraduate	94.8	1.7	4.1
5.	Professional/technical training	95.7	1.7	2.4

(d) makes the mobility of educated people possible in the country and abroad; and
(e) is a status symbol.

Regarding the usefulness of language in professions, it is observed that those occupations which do not require any academic training are thought to need only the regional language and Hindi, while professions which require academic/technical training such as medical, legai practice, university teaching, engineering etc. demand proficiency in English. However, certain occupations which do not require academic training and which are not considered high on the scale of prestige either were also thought to require English for success, for example, field requiring skilled workers and businessmen. These responses show a bias towards the usefulness of English. The survey shows that people want to retain English in India for utilitarian purposes and not for any cultural identification with the English speaking people (Prasher 1979b). It is clear that the motivation for learning English in India is instrumental rather than integrative. The evidences show that they are aware of its practical uses and no one has desire to become one with the English culture.

'Decline' of Hindi and strong tendency, as recorded in Khubchandani (1967), to record languages and dialects of the Hindi group as separate languages, might have caused the leaning towards English. Total number of L_2 speakers in English and 14 major Indian languages recognised in the Constitution (1961 Census) throughout the country is hundreds of thousands. Language-wise figures show that number of L_2 speakers are maximum in English followed by Hindi. In Bihar there are about 4,982,615 Maithili speakers in 1961 (Language and Society 1969).

In the last few years number of public schools increased surprisingly. In Darbhanga municipal area, each municipal ward has at least one and, in some cases, more than one public schools. Even people of low income group want to send their wards to these schools. This increase in enrolment in English medium schools occurs despite free teaching in government schools.

Despite this increasing zeal for English, students use Hindi or Maithili for intra-ethnic communication. Approximately 60 per cent of the population speak Maithili as their L_1 and rest of them speak Hindi, Urdu, Bhojpuri, Magadhi, Bengali, etc. as their first language. In general, Hindi is still popular in day-to-day life. English is hardly used in the performance of chores. The enthusiasm is limited to classrooms only, and very few of the local public school pupils attain proficiency in English despite the large number opting for it in the secondary schools. The students who do matriculation after 10 years of formal instruction in English have an average reading vocabulary of only 1,000 words and no more than 5 per cent of these could read even simple book in English. Therefore, at the university level, English cannot be dependably used as the base language. Few of university libraries hold substantial collections of current texts in English, most students can obtain the information in these volumes only if their professors can read the books and summarise the contents in lectures in Hindi or through bazar notes in Hindi.

These disappointing results of English teaching focus our attention to some in-built problems in the education system. Class-rooms do not have enough teaching equipments and poor proficiency of English teachers unable to cope with the demand of teaching. Due to poor salary of school and college teachers they are busy in other side businesses or tuitions which affect their sincerity towards teaching. Not surprisingly, the best teachers with the highest proficiency in English often leave this profession for employment in high salaried private or government jobs.

However, poor study and teaching conditions alone do not adequately explain the low proficiency in English at places like Darbhanga. The majority of students have very little opportunity to converse in or listen to the language except in the classroom. Even the popular programmes on Indian Radio and TV have negligible contents of English language. The serious programmes like talks, discussions, reportage in English are held back for late-night broadcast or beaming.

A small percentage of students, nevertheless, become proficient in English. They often come form elite and affluent family background and have their early education in public schools outside Bihar. Private institutes, particularly English-spoken institutes, are available in large numbers for aspiring learners from the middle and lower-middle families to prepare for banking and other services. It is noted that English is seldom used for connected discourse when these students communicate among themselves. Rather its use is restricted to code mixing and using English words and phrases in their conversation.

A survey has been made to record attitude variables. Table below shows different attitudes shown by the students of different faculties

Table 3.4: Student Attitude of Different Faculty Towards English

S. No.	*Faculty*	*Percentage*
1.	Science	77.9
2.	Commerce	56.08
3.	Arts	3.01

The students in the faculty of science have the most favourable attitude towards English (77.9 per cent). On the contrary, the students in the faculty of arts (3.01 per cent) have a very low percentage. Students in the faculty of commerce show a greater interest (56.08 per cent) in English.

Nativisation in Darbhanga

Post-independence changes in the contexts of culture and situation spread all over India. English is thought to be a symbol of status. Its utility and the multilingual character of the country have created a ready market for English. The range and depth of English in the linguistic repertoires of this speech fellowship have expanded. In accordance with these varying degrees of range and depth, the forms and functions of English have been diversely nativised. This nativisation has been realised in linguistic deviations from native speaker norms as opposed to deficiencies (errors and mistakes), as discussed earlier.

According to types of nativised features and the frequency with which these features appear when used by "educated" speakers of particular linguistic area, a speech can be divided into three 'sociolects' – an acrolect, a mesolect and a basilect. These speakers use the acrolect, mesolect and basilect for talking and writing in formal, semiformal and casual situations respectively. Each of these sociolects is marked linguistically by the degree to which its features have been nativised.

The Acrolect

The acrolect is the standard sub-variety of Standard Indian English, (henceforth SIE). The standard model for a variety of English can be defined as the linguistic forms of that variety that are normally used in formal speaking and writing by speakers who have been educated in that variety of English. It is the accepted model for government, business and academic writings and for public speaking before an audience or on radio or TV. The acrolect is generally used by the educated speaking in formal speaking or writing situations, such as university lectures, government meetings and commercial meetings or preparing manuscripts. It contains few deviations from the norms of standard English in the native speaker variety and is generally intelligible to educated speakers of other varieties of English.

There is no such big business or Central government offices or centre for higher academic activities in the area of our study and thus acrolect does not come within the purview of our study.

The Mesolect

The middle range of the SIE speech, mesolect, is considerably more nativised than the acrolect. It is used by educated SIE speakers in semiformal situations, such as shopping in fashionable department stores with smart sales-girls or in informal conversations with strangers who also speak SIE. The area of our study does not offer scope for the study of mesolect.

The Basilect

The range of the speakers of Maithili English, (henceforth SME), continuum exhibiting the most nativisation is the basilect, which contains so many deviations from the native speaker varieties that it creates problems of intelligibility for outsider.

We find in the survey that our learners aspire for an acrolect and/ or mesolect for their purpose. In classes the emphasis is on acrolect but not on its spoken form but in its written form which are reflected in their speech on informal occasions. Actually, this speech community (Maithili) speaks mostly in their mother tongue inside and outside family for most of their work. Even Hindi is hardly used on very few occasions. So there arises the question of the status of English in these domains. Only professionals like doctors, bureaucrats use English. But they are only restricted to formal occasions. Hence, they provide clues in terms of regional accent, which is reflected in their speech (Chaudhary 1989).

Apart from their accent, their speech contains a rumber of features which are unrelated to regional variation (Yule 1985: Chapter XX).

(a) Geographical area, and
(b) Other social factors.

The patterns of change in the use and usage of English can be identified into two heads:

(i) Context of culture
(ii) Context of situation

Context of Culture

Context of culture can be studied under three variables:

1. Political variable
2. Economic variable
3. Socio-cultural variable.

Political Variable

Due to political interference in framing educational policy, the status of English as a major subject of study has been seriously affected.

Economic Variable

Economically this area is backward. It has no industry or business or trade worth the name. Contact with the wide world outside is very narrow. Because of lack of direct communicational facility by rail and the routine disruption of road communication by flood for periods upto 6 to 8 weeks in a year, this area has remained cut-off from the mainstream of development. Except for the "creamy layer" in the citizenry consisting of medical practitioners and wealthy members of business community, the basic pattern is rural agrarian.

Socio-cultural Variable

The population is mixed but Maithili language is dominant in and around Darbhanga. Hence, this language is used in almost every domain. Arpita Mishra (1985) in "Language Abroad: A Socio-linguistic Study of Conversations in Interethnic Settings", says that difficulties in communication do not necessarily disappear as learner gains control of basic English grammar and vocabulary. The question is not simply one of foreign accent, but there is something more than that. Our students' writings may meet the requirements of English grammar, yet we often find that the English spoken or written by an Indian is not intelligible or understood by a native speaker of the language. They are unintelligible not only due to the accent and stress pattern but more importantly in their assumptions about the situation and about appropriate behaviour and intentions within it. They differ in their way of giving information and in structuring an argument, in their way of speaking, viz., the use of a different set of linguistic conventions (such as pitch, tone of voice etc.) to give emphasis to signal connections and changes in the focus of the argument. These are some of the areas in which we clearly and systematically differ from the native speaker. They have different experience of culture, social setup and knowledge of social norms and customs.

Culture is the context in which a person lives, thinks and feels. It is a collective identity of which each of us is an integral part.

M. Kundu (1982) describes culture as a force which guides the life style of people.

A language grows in the culture and bears the imprint of the culture and the fact has always created problem for L_2 teachers. There exist a lot of differences between the culture of the learner and the culture of the people whose language he learns. In fact, what is acceptable to one culture is not acceptable to the another. Rather, it is interpreted as something which is quite opposite to the culture of the learner.

Paramanik (1988) has pointed out some interesting affective variables related to learning English. The Negro people, for instance, show respect by not looking directly in the eyes of the person with whom they talk. This is a mark of respect for Negro people. But this is interpreted by white teachers as lack of interest. In India begging apology during the course of conversation occurs very rarely. But it is recurrently present in English culture in the form of 'excuse me', 'beg your pardon', and 'pardon please', etc. Such queries are often faced by the researcher in her language class. At times it is difficult for the L_2 learner to conceive some social traditions such as marriage, table manners and religious rituals. They appear as a cultural shock to the L_2 learners, particularly to those who had remained shut in culturally and economically.

Other than this language shock, there is another problem which is related to correct naming of objects and ideas. In our native languages, we feel dissatisfied when we do not get correct words to express ourselves. At this point our learners face a sense of insufficiency in the language.

Words often carry with them visual images, but a word in the L_2 may carry an image that is quite different from the one carried by the L_1. For instance, words like 'butterfly' or 'lady's finger' may bear a different visual image for the L_2 learner. The use of a L_2 may cause a sense of shame and insufficiency which affects the self-confidence or what is called "narcissistic gratification" of the learner.

Communication is a two-party transaction in which both parties have to negotiate at every step in order to reach a mutually agreeable interpretive meaning of different speech utterances and of discourse at large. Arpita Mishra (1985) shows how members of two different social systems fail to understand each other because they are members of two different social systems; hence have different experiences and views. The use of different prosodic features to signal emphasis complicate the matter further. The article shows that interpretation of communicative intent is not predictable on the basis of referential meaning alone. Instead, context, social presuppositions, knowledge of the world and of the individual's background all play an important role in the process of message. Linguistic pragmatics assume that given a stretch of speech and a rough specification of the contextual setting in which it was produced, speaker and hearer can readily agree on what is intended. What happens, participants can understand the referential meaning of individual sentences but they differ in their interpretation of the communicative intent.

Context of Situation

Apart from context of culture, there are context of situation which affects the teaching-learning situation. Fishman (1972) summarises these variables which are relevant to the actual use of language listed below:

1. Setting or scene : time and place, psychological setting and cultural definition of the type of scene.
2. Participants or personnel : addressor-addressee-audience.
3. Ends : ends and goals in view and in outcome.
4. Art characteristics : the form and content of what is said.
5. Key : tone, manner or spirit in which one act is done.
6. Instrumentalities : channel and code or sub-code.
7. Norms of interaction and interpretation.
8. Genres : traditional categories of speech, acts and events.

Fishman (1972) defines the smallest socio-linguistic unit as the speech, which is part of a larger speech event such as a conversation, prayer or lecture. What demanded from the learner is to show connections between speech acts and events and types of languages. Such variables consist of role relationships recognised in that particular community : husband/wife, father/son, employer/employee, friend/enemy etc. These relationships are more stable hence can be learnt easily but some are more invariant, for instance, shopkeeper/customers. The situational contexts in time and place may similarly affect the situations.

There are a number of sociolinguistic studies dealing with

contextually conditioned variation, like:

Fishman 1968, 1972,
Gumperz and Hymes 1972,
Hymes 1964, 1967, 1977,
Labov 1970, 1972, and
Pride and Holmes 1972.

Glaser (1969) emphasises that these situational variables may affect the choice of linguistic features at all levels of language. She also cites Trojan (1952) to connect intonation patterns with subjective situational features: surprise, joy, disappointment, disgust. Thus, there may be links between psychological motivation and the phonetic surface shape of an utterance. This one again brings up the problem of the relation between contextual and paralinguistic feature.

The speech form is initially a function of a given social arrangement. Therefore, different speech forms or codes symbolize the form of the social relationship and regulate the nature of the speech encounters and create for the speaker's different orders of relevance and relation.

The social class structure influences work and educational roles and deeply penetrates the structure of like experiences within the family. The class system has deeply marked the distribution of knowledge within society. The forms of socialisation orient the child towards speech codes within control access to relatively context tied or relatively context independent meanings. Bernstein (1973) argues that elaborated codes orient their users towards universal users to particularistic meanings, whereas restricted codes orient, sensitize their users to particularistic meanings: the linguistic realisations of the two orders are different, and so are the social relationships which realise them.

Sapir and Firth have pointed out from different points of view that the closer the identifications of speakers and the greater the range of shared interest, the more probable that the speech will take a specific form. The form of these social relations are acting selectively on the meanings to be verbally realised. In these relationships the intent of the other person can be taken for granted as the speech is played against a backdrop of common assumptions, common history, common interests. As a result, there is less need to raise meanings to the level of explicitness or elaboration. And a reduced need to make explicit through syntactic choices, the logical structure of the communication. If speaker wishes to individualise his communication, he is to do this by varying the expressive associates of the speech. In such situations he may be more concerned with how something is said and when it is said – even silence takes on a variety of meanings. Often in these encounters the speech cannot be understood apart from the context and the context cannot be read by those who do not share the history of relationship. The symbolic form of the communication is condensed yet the specific cultural history of relationship is alive in its form.

Our students do not have specific cultural history and are unaware of their relationship, they either misunderstand or do not comprehend the speech. Since they cannot manage the role, they cannot produce the appropriate speech. Therefore, when teaching them English language, they demand for more explicitness. They need a very precise instruction to hypothesize in that particular context. When they are asked to associate a series of words, their responses show considerable diversity, both from meaning and from class of the stimulus words. A greater range of alternatives is possible to candidates for selection. But closely controlled linguistic socialisation may point them towards both the grammatical significance of the stimulus word and towards a tight logical ordering of semantic space. The consequences limit their imagination through the tightness of the frame which these interpretive rule create. For these reasons only, the speech shows a considerable deviation from the native speaker's normal speech.

Nelson Brook (1960) points out "in the popular mind language is what is written in books and learnt in school". The central band of the language spectrum, the audio-lingual, is primary and generative, while the other two bands the gestural-visual and the graphic material are derivative. But this central aspect is very often neglected due to many reasons discussed earlier under different heads. We teach in our class the other two 'bands'; more importance is attached to these derivatives. That is why, when our students complete their MA English course, their terminal level behaviour is not up to the mark, hence they hesitate to talk in that language.

A successful L_2 learning entails a complete personal participation of the learner. Learning a L_2 is not merely an intellectual activity, nor the outcome of habit formation, because a total physical, intellectual linguistic message. Brown (1981) is of the opinion that language is inextricably bound up in virtually every aspect of human behaviour.

Cohen (1977) suggests that the students, who have less tolerance for ambiguity, cannot listen more attentively, therefore, they are confused by the linguistic input. They are unable to comprehend it well and hence can attend to it much less efficiently.

The unsuccessful L_2 learning are due to affective blocks of different kinds which are caused by a wider dimension of socio-cultural variations. Taxonomy of affective variables in L_2 learning is as follows:

(a) Self centric factors
(b) Inter-personal factors
(c) Personality factors
(d) Motivation
(e) Attitude
(f) Socio-cultural factors — Cultural shock
Language shock
Cultural stress

[For detail please *see* T.K. Pramanic 1988, CIEFL and Eloise Pearson (1988)].

Rivers (1983) finds that L_2 learner often compares the L_2 system with his L_1. If he finds similarity in any aspect he thinks that other systems of the language must correspond to his own language system. For example, 'gender' makes a clear and identifiable semantic distinction in both the languages (Maithili and English). On this basis it is very hard for them to conceive the idea that other parts of speech do not have identical rules. Although this has been explained to them, they still have to make a conscious mental effort to keep this all pervading concept in mind while they apply lower level inflectional rules in all kinds of positions and relationships. Specific errors that these learners make in omitting the morphemes indicating these agreements may be interpreted as intralingual, as simplification, or as overgeneralisation errors, whereas the basic problem is an interlingual conceptual contrast. The insecurity and uncertainty about the extent of applicability of new rules is a distinct psychological phenomenon from that of overgeneralisation.

Effects of Culture and Deviations from the Norm

A. Adakou, D. Britten, B. Fahsi in "Design Decisions on the Cultural Content of a Secondary English Course for Morocco" (1990) discuss four separate understanding of 'culture' that a language teaching may involve. They are:

(a) The aesthetic sense,
(b) The sociological sense,
(c) The semantic sense, and
(d) The pragmatic (or sociolinguistic) sense.

Out of these four types, last two are necessary for the achievement of a measure of communicative competence. The other two are to foster international understanding and for enjoyment of great literary works, cinema, media, etc. of Europe. These two aspects embody the organisation and nature of family, life, interpersonal relations, work and leisure, customs and institutions, etc.

In our texts the first two aspects of culture are dominant and last two aspects are often neglected. Since many of our teachers and students are ignorant of aesthetic and sociocultural aspects of European culture, they find themselves helpless at this juncture.

Now in the light of above discussed socio-cultural factors, we try to see the texts prescribed. For intermediate students, four text-books are prescribed:

1. *Prose selection*—It has been prose pieces out of which at least two do not fit in the Indian context.
2. *Poetry selection*—There are eighteen poetry pieces, in which only one is an Anglo-Indian poem. Rest are written by British and American poets. Their tone and attitudes, which constitute meaning, are neither appropriate nor understood.
3. *Five one act plays*—Five plays are prescribed out of which only one play 'Rana Pratap' has an Indian context.
4. *Lamb's Tales from Shakespeare/tales*—Old and new stories are prescribed but most of them have unfamiliar cultural context.

On the basis of texts prescribed, our student's language competence is measured on these components given below:

Paper I — This comprises of text books, two (prose and poetry pieces) for detailed study and two (drama and story) for non-detailed study. The evaluating items comprise and demand on the part of students' familiarity with the contents prescribed.

Paper II — This relates exclusively to the composition and usage of grammatical items and translation of a given passage.

All these demand students' descriptive skill and there is no place for communicative skill. Their answer scripts show that following area of errors/deviations:

Phonological—No provision is made for reading texts and dictation in the classroom. It is found that they have some misconception. An overall analysis of their speech it is found that phonological features include those phonological features which cut across the political and/or geographical boundaries of the area. The competence of the speakers of English varies so much that one is prone to find a kind of confusion (Kachru 1983). The phonetic and phonological deviations are essentially determined by the phonetic and phonological structures of the L_1. These deviations are of two types:

(a) Those of segmental phonemes, and
(b) Those of non-segmental phonemes.

Segmental Phonemes

It is well known fact that dialects of a language differ mainly in the pronunciation of certain vowels and consonants. The standard varieties of spoken English differ mainly in some of their vowels and consonants causing unintelligibility. Many structures or phonemes of L_1 are absent in L_2 (in this case, English) or the structures may be 'identical', yet there may be systematic differences. We find that CVC morpheme structure is found in the two languages. Thus in the restricted sense this language may be considered 'identical' with

English at the phonetic level. However, these vary in the elements which operate in the system (*cf.* Barron 1961a and 1961b, Pandit 1964).

Very common mispronunciations are:

(a) English labio-dental fricatives as bilabial stops according to the Hindi/Maithili sounds.
(b) Dental fricatives pronounced as dental stops.
(c) Non-distinction between the alveolar and palato-alveolar sibilants.
(d) The tendency to pronounce the voiced alveolar fricative as palato-alveolar affricate:

These systemic differences are not only found in its elements but may occur in terms of distribution also. It is possible that the two languages have 'identical' phonetic elements, but these shared sounds may operate in different systems. Both in Maithili and English *sk, st, sp* clusters are present. Structurally these elements are shared but systematically they differ. In many varieties of Hindi *sk, sp, st* do not occur in word initial position. Hence they are prone to add a centralised front, unrounded vowel /*i*/ before these consonant clusters sounding as 'istation' 'ischool', 'ispeak', 'istall', 'ispecial' (for detail please *see* B.B. Kuchru 1983).

What happens, usually unconsciously, is that the most approximate sound is substituted from the phonological inventory of L_1. In fact, every language has its own rules for clustering of consonants and vowels and its feature changes according to the place where it occurs (for detail please see Chaudhary, 1989).

English has unpredictable orthographic form. Its orthographic form does not correspond to its phonetic form as is found in most of the Indian subvarieties of languages. This unpredictability causes much problem to the learners. Double-letter words like 'marriage', 'robber', etc. are often misspelt. Due to unfamiliarity with the orthographic form they very often write two separate words together. (See *Appendix* B_2).

They have special problem with the vowels and diphthongs. Many vowels of English are not found in Indian languages particularly diphthongs and central vowels. That's why, they have difficulty in making distinction between (in spoken from) pairs like the following:

/i:/	/i/	/e/	/ei/	/ei/	/e/
beat	bit	fell	fail	gate	get
eat	it	let	late	bale	bell
feet	fit	met	mate	tale	tell
feel	fill	test	taste	main	men
sleep	slip	west	waste	mate	met

(For detail please see Thomas 1992).

Our students often tend to transfer their L_1 habits when they read any piece. In most of the Indian languages each sound is pronounced, therefore, they read 'suddenly' as 'सूडेनली', listening as 'लिस्टेनिंग'.

Actually what happens when a learner, says Choudhary (1989), learns "new items or rules only when they appear to him as markedly different from the ones he knows and/or when he feels compiled to learn them. In all other cases he would abstract the new items too in terms of the existing ones. This latter phenomenon seems to have overtaken orthography in ME".

Other features which are common in ME are:

(a) L_1 pull.
(b) Restructuring of English words.
(c) Prosodic processing — Lengthening
Reduction
Addition
Elimination of vowels
Gemination of consonants.

Non-segmental Phonemes

The main phonological features of IE and its varieties, which separate it from the AE/BE, are not necessarily the deviations in the segmental phonemes but the deviations in stress, rhythm, intonation, etc. Pass'e (1947), DeLanerolle (1953), Gopal Krishnan (1960), Hai and Ball (1961) and Sisson (1971) have discussed certain non-segmental features of some varieties of SAE. Hai and Ball deals with regards to Bengali, whereas Gopalkrishnan's observation is the English spoken by South Indians. Usmani deals with Urdu and Taylor's study is based on widely spoken North Indian Language (Hindi). North Indian English features are not different from Dravidian English. They conclude that the underlying reasons for the deviation in stress are following:

(a) All the main SALs are syllables-timed languages, as opposed to English which is a stress-timed language.
(b) South Asian rhythm in SAE is based on arranging long and short syllables and not stress and unstressed syllables.

There is a strong tendency to give full value to auxiliary verb forms written as contraction and to accord them a relatively strong stress as well. Besides this, there is a strong tendency to break up grammatical units arbitrarily within sentences. Thus violating the confines of 'sense group' and placing a strong stress on words other than those normally found to have sense stress. There is a general lack of recognition of the primary/tertiary pattern of stress for compound nouns as opposed to the secondary/primary pattern used for free noun/noun combination. They tended to place stress on the suffix itself.

Syntax

Sinclair and Couthard (1974) examined the structure of classroom discourse and found that it differed in a number of ways from discourse in other situations.

U. Weinreich (1963) says pragmatics is part of semantics to the extent that its features are codeable, codeability implying the presence of formal markers already described in the grammar. Labels such as 'command', 'request', etc. are of course by no means easy to define. What might be a 'command' for the speaker or writer might have the force of a 'request' or merely a piece of 'advice' for the listener or reader. Moreover, for any person what a 'command' is will depend on what a 'request' is, and a 'suggestion' etc. There would still appear to be sets of terms here amounting to semantic fields in their own right.

Martinet (1962) draws our attention to certain basic facts about language. He points out that no community is linguistically homogeneous. Many people belong to two or more than two language communities and concurrently different styles of the same language.

He further observes: "Language varies because it suits the varying needs of man. That is diversity is the very nature of language.

B.K. Lal (1981) finds another factor, which causes diversity, that is interference of L_1. The notion of 'interference' is derived from the behaviouristic theory of learning according to which learning involves a passive process of habit formation. Interference results from the fact that old habits are transferred to a new task.

It has been assumed that when a L_2 is learned with regard to the L_1 learning, it is filtered through the learner's language acquisition system which has already been modified by structure of the first language. When the structure of L_1 and those of L_2 are different, negative transfer or interference of L_1 structures occur in L_2 learning resulting in deviant constructions or error in L_2; when L_1 and L_2 structures are similar, positive transfer or facilitation takes place leading to immediate learning of L_2 structure. In this connection Weinreich's (1953) hypothesis is that "the greater the difference between the systems (of two languages) *i.e.*, the more numerous the mutually exclusive forms and patterns in each, the greater is the learning problem and the potential area of interference. For instance, the absence of article in many Indian sub-varieties as opposed to that of English (see Dustoor 1954, 1955). This is reflected in the samples collected from answer scripts. (Samples were collected in the course of evaluating answer scripts of Inter Science examinee 1993 – evaluation centre C.M. College, Darbhanga from May, 10 to May 20, 1993.) Sentences and passage containing * mark are taken from the answer scripts (please see Appendix B_2).

(a) *Error in the use of article:*

*1. Sun and moon are in sky.

*2. This is an unique opportunity.

Since Maithili or Hindi has no articles so students feel confused in their application.

(b) *Wrong word order:*

*1. The lyre musical instrument Orpheus play.

*2. Crime had the daughters of Danas committed, who had killed their husbands on their marriage night.

(c) *Formation of questions:*

*1. What is your preparation for examination.
*2. Have you come alone?
*3. Why not your younger brother?
*4. Is something especial or general.
*5. How is your mummy and papa and other family members.
*6. You went to see a film last night?

It is clear from the above examples that their confusions are for appropriate wh-words, inappropriate use of auxiliary verbs, omission of verb (auxiliary or main or both, omission of mark of interrogation, and arrangement of sentence structure have similarity with sentence structure of L_1 as in sentences 4 and 5.

(d) *Wrong use of tense:*

*1. I have come here yesterday.
*2. He come round use medicine.
*3. It finded in pleasure and sorrow.

(e) *Concord:*

*1. Neither he nor I is willing to go.
*2. A hundred rupees are a lot of money.

(f) *Use of two adjectives:*

*1. Library is a very big friend of man.
*2. Library is a very good friend of man.
*3. With due respect and humble submission I have ....
*4. I have come to know that my mother is very very ill.

Above samples clearly show learner's confusion about the system of rules underlying language learning. Since the two languages are structurally so different that it causes many confusions to a L_2 learner (for observation of such errors please see Kachru 1983). In learning a language the individual acquires the system of rules underlying that language which enables him to produce and understand sentences not produced before. Observations made by Kindersley (1938),V. Saraswathi (1978), A.K. Sharma (1992) and many others found that the area which create problems to our learners are mainly S-V concord, complex sentence formation and particularly verb forms. In the use of verbs, the main problems are:

(a) in construction of be + verb + ing, thus violating the selectional restriction applicable to such constructions in the native varieties where the members of the sub-class of verbs such as 'hear' and 'see' do not occur in the progressive tense (*see* Kindersley 1938).
(b) in the reflexive verbs (*e.g.,* enjoy, exert) the reflexive pronoun is omitted.
(c) In place of transitive verb, intransitive verbs are used.
(d) In constructions such as verb + particle (*e.g.,* dispose of) the particle is added to such verbs as normally do not take the particle (*e.g.,* eat off, rear off).

Other areas which cause more problems are phrasal verbs (Richard Side 1990). It creates problem because they are so many and the combination of verb and particle seems so often completely random. Teachers advise students to memorise the lot. Phrasal verbs have a confusing number of combination and many of them have more than one meaning. The meaning of idiomatic phrasal verbs do not appear to be the sum of the two (or three) parts. More often there is no direct equivalent of phrasal verbs. The other problem is L_1 difference. No Indian languages, particularly Maithili, have prepositions or particles. Therefore, the problem is the interference of linguistic as well as conceptual which culturally varies. Absence of these items often causes problems to readers and learners of L_2 ["Ins and Outs of prepositions" in *Frontline* August (17-30) 1991].

S. Sivaraman (1992) says Idioms function as single pieces and their meanings cannot be calculated by adding up the separate meanings of the parts. They normally do not admit any freedom. But due to unawareness of this fact our students often either replace any one of its word or according to their cultural concept, they use it for another meaning. Adverbial – adjectival phrase is so 'deeply embedded in the essential nature and character of idiomatic English that its misuse often distorts the real flavour of the language. Sometimes our learners use reduplication of a word as in

*My mother is *very very* ill.
Her hair is *very very* long.

They use it for emphasis and sometimes to indicate the continuation of the process.

Indian languages have "Case" and relationship between the parts of speech indicated by the case markers. But English has no functional realisation of use, except the possessive case. Therefore, our learners often confuse case with prepositions. Case markers in Hindi/Maithili are at post-position.

Our students have a tendency towards using complex noun and verb phrases and rather long sentences. It is obvious through the sample given below:

> *With due respect and humble submission, I have to say that I am bona fide boarder in the college hostel. It is extremely regrettable to inform you that my father has fallen seriously ill. My mother has called me through her letter to come home soon.

Noam Chomsky (1965) says that rules of the structure of language are 'independent' of the rules of language use. His capacity to form and understand sentences of that language is his linguistic competence.

Le Page (1968a, 1979) says, "Each individual creates the system for his verbal behaviours so that they shall resemble those of the group or groups with which from time to time he may wish to be identified."

What we find that each group potentially influences the creation of the individual verbal system as each group gives him a different experience of language. Different languages within his verbal system can be treated as elements of a system controlled by an individual. This variety may have different manifestations. A single utterance may include items from several languages known to a speaker (Chaudhary 1981). The learner may be careful enough to note the differences, but may ignore or de-emphasize the areas that are structurally similar but used to be learnt. Though there may be areas of syntactic similarities in two languages, the socio-linguistic choice governing their usage may differ. That is, what may be appropriate in one language may not only be inappropriate but unnatural in another (Sawhney 1980). For instance complementizer marker /कि/ki/appears in the beginning of the interrogative retains in Hindi, but English deletes them obligatorily. If this fact is not taken note of, one may end up saying sentences such as (1) and (2) which our learners have actually used in narration exercise.

1. I asked him that why was he late?
2. I asked him that why are you coming late these days?

Most typical of the movement of items from their respective linguistic bundle to form a new structural relationship is relevant in our learners. This phenomenon is called code-switching and code-mixing. Verma (1976), Kachru (1978) and Gumperz (1982) studied this aspect with regards to Indian languages.

Speakers do borrow items from English when they are speaking Hindi or Maithili or Maithili Hindi mixed-code. For example:

1. English : Ekà:si : Men je *census* bhel rahai ....
   (The census conducted in 1981......).
2. ek a:dmi:Pu:re *team* ko *final* tak Pahuncha : Sakaɩa : hai.
   (One man can take a team to the final).

(adapted from Jha 1993).

(For detail please see Qaiser Zoha Alam 1987, S.K. Sawhney 1980, S.C. Chaudhary 1981 and S.N. Jha, 1993.)

Social value of language reveals itself in all manner of socially motivated verbal behaviour. Possibilities exist not only for seemingly straightforward and stable code-switching, but also for the acceptance of another form of speech in partial or complete replacement. Then there is the possibility of borrowing items and features, either in an unassimilated form or in an assimilated form. All these behaviours can occur together or separately, and not only language but also dialects and styles or varieties of language may be involved (J.B. Pride 1971).

Lexis

It could be studied on account of two characteristic features:

(a) Nonshared with those varieties of English which are used as L_1 (register restricted and culture bound).
(b) Transferred from the Indian languages to the L_1 variety of English.

First variety is more common in our students. They often translate words literally in English.

For example 'village home', 'illing father', 'bona fide boarder', 'extremely regrettable' etc.

The other type of deviations are that of collocational. This may be of three types:

(a) Grammatical deviations from L_1 variety of English. This would account as ignorant English.
(b) Loan shifts or lexis bound translations show the transfer of fixed collocations of learners (Indian/Maithili) into English.
(c) Contextual deviation. It involves a semantic shift.

In Darbhanga loan shifts or lexis-bound translations are more common. It is obvious from the examples below:

(*1) If the wheels *works* against each other, the cart cannot moves.
(*2) The farmer *hit upon aplain* to teach them the importance of unity.
(*3) Respectfully big to say that my father been suffering from fevor for a month at my *village home*.
(*4) So that I may go home and see my *illing father*.
(*5) I shall be granted to you *for doing this*.
(*6) My mother has called me *through her letter*.
(*7) At present, I have to look after the deteriorating health of my *old ailing father*.

Over and above, such grammatical or spelling errors, another typical error committed by Indian/Maithili learners of English is the omission of courtesy words like please, thank you. On the other hand, in Indian languages including Maithili there is an abundance of polite forms of language corresponding to social norms and conventions for which English equivalents are not available. Indian languages have an excess of polite forms like blessings and good wishes for younger people, respect and honour for greeting senior people, certain verbal inflexions to denote the status of the person addressed as also the relation and attitude of the speaker. Another tendency which is very common among Indians is phrase mongering (see Greffin 1934) which is determined by the structure of L_1 and also by various types of collocational deviations. Excessive use of cliches is very common in Indian English as "better imagined than described" (easily imagined), "do the needful" etc. Deletion is another common factor in Indian English. There is natural tendency to reduce a syntactic unit of a higher rank in the L_1 variety of English to a lower rank in Indian English. In Indian English many nominal formations of modifier + head + qualifier (MHQ) structure are reduced to (MH) structure (Kachru 1965). A large number of such phrases are produced by rank reduction. They involve first the process of deletion and then permutation of the lexical items, such as the following nominal groups of English:

(a) 'an address of welcome' reduced to 'welcome address'
(b) 'A bunch of keys' reduced to 'key bunch'.

Goffin finds that in spoken form of Indian variety there is an over use of opening "well". The other point where learners have confusion is regarding 'yes – no'. What happens in Indian languages the choice of 'yes' or 'no' in a question depends on

(a) the form of the question, and
(b) the facts of the situation.

If both (a) and (b) have the same polarity (both positive or negative) the answer is positive. If, on the other hand, the polarity is not the same (say the question is in the positive and the situation is negative, or the converse) the answer is negative. But the selection of 'yes' or 'no' depends on the facts of the situation. If the situation is positive, the answer is yes if it is negative, the answer is no. This area often creates problem in communication.

In both spoken and written mediums Indian users tend to use certain lexical and grammatical constructions which either have been dropped or are less frequent in modern English. Mathai comments:

"Indian learned a great part of his English from books. Indian English was, therefore, always inclined to be bookish .... often freely garnished with phrases and patterns of expression taken from the great writers" (Mathai 1951).

Hence spoken language does not sound conversational, as the spoken medium has been seldom taught as an academic discipline in Indian educational system. That is why, our learners are not made conscious of the characteristics of spoken English (see Kachru 1982a).

Indians are bilingual in the sense that they are using English as a complementary language in typically Indian contexts. An Indian bilingual's use of English is conditioned by his cultural background. In linguistic terms a study of a language contact situation involves a study of transfer at different levels. The types of transfer may be discussed in terms of:

(a) transfer of context,
(b) transfer of formal items, and
(c) transfer of form/context components.

Transfer of context involves the transfer of certain contextual units which may be non-belonging elements of the culture of L_2 such as caste system, social and religious taboos, notions of superiority and inferiority and the like. Transfer of formal items may be of two types:

(a) Formal items from different ranks may be transferred from L_1 to L_2 (sentences, clauses, phrases, fixed collocation, compounds) for example—
   (i) bow my forehead
   (ii) turmeric ceremony
   (iii) return back
(b) L_1 meaning may be transferred to L_2 items. For instance the term "brother-in-law" has one restricted meaning in B.E. as a kinship term, in IE it has acquired three distinct meanings as a term of (i) abuse, (ii) affection or intimacy, and (iii) kinship.

Socially determined speech functions such as modes of address, reference, greetings, blessings, prayers, abuses/curses are related to the Indian context of culture. In Indian languages, there are fixed formal exponents for these contexts and these may be transferred to L_2 for those contextual units which are absent in the culture of L_2. For instance:

> "Hello Mohan *jee*"
> "O! *come come*"
> "What are you doing these days *silently*"
> "Is something *special or general*"

emphasis, different pause are possible. Unawareness to these phrasal pause makes their speech a monotonous and nearly syllable timed rhythm, different from standard English makes incomprehensible to those not used to this style of speaking.

Word stress is the most erratic aspect of English phonology. But in multi-cultural, multi-disciplinary situations, such as when we meet formally, a deviant word stress can inhibit understanding. Experiments have proved that people can differ in the actual realisation of vowels and consonants, and they might still be understood by listeners, if they use standard word stress (S. Choudhary, 1993).

They do not have control over different speech styles and registers in the language and consequently fail to vary their speech in a way what is situationally appropriate. All these give English a typical feature of the place. This discussion of the uses of English in India in general, and in Darbhanga in particular, demonstrates how in a performance variety English undergoes considerable nativisation in the contexts of culture and situation in which it is used. This variety of English has its distinctive feature which is somewhat deviant from SIE.

4

Analysis of the Data

Technicalia

Out of total of fifteen colleges and five inter-schools, in and around the corporation limit of the city of Darbhanga, five colleges, which are recently affiliated, have been left out due to negligible number of students studying English in these institutions.* Five inter-schools and ten colleges, in and around Darbhanga, were selected for study. These schools and colleges have, on their rolls, students hailing from both rural and urban backgrounds. The standard of institutions was decided on the basis of students' proficiency level required for admission to the intermediate course, the establishment year of the institution and the general public opinion. These schools and colleges are:

Schools — All are Inter-Schools

(a) Raj Inter School
(b) Zila School
(c) L.R. Girls School
(d) M.L. Academy
(e) Marwari School.

**Note*: Institutions left out are:

1. Rana Pratap College
2. Mahesh Prasad Singh College
3. Mithila Mahila College
4. Jalan College
5. Mahatma Gandhi College
6. Navodaya School (following C.B.S.E. course is also left out).

Colleges

(a)	C.M. College	Constituent unit of the university
(b)	C.M. Science College	Constituent unit of the university
(c)	M.R.M. College	Constituent unit of the university
(d)	Marwari College	Constituent unit of the university
(e)	Millat College	Constituent unit of the university
(f)	K.S. College	Constituent unit of the university
(g)	M.L.S.M. College	Constituent unit of the university
(h)	M.K. College	Constituent unit of the university
(i)	N. Jha Mahila College	Affiliated to L.N.M. University
(j)	Lohia Charan Singh College	Affiliated to L.N.M. University

Students studying in these schools and colleges represent a wide range in terms of socio-economic conditions and their performance levels.

The present survey is restricted only to the Intermediate (+2) students because intermediate course is the crucial gateway, branching off in different vocational careers. Approximately 350,000 students appeared for intermediate examinations in 1991 (Bihar Intermediate Education Council, budget estimates 1991-1992, Patna BEC). At entry level these students represent a wide range of ability in English due to their socio-cultural and educational backgrounds (A.K. Sharma, 1992).

Collection of Data

To collect relevant information following methods and equipments are used:

1. Questionnaire (for students and teachers).
2. Personal interviews (with students and teachers).
3. Language laboratory (P.G. Department of English, L.N.M.U.).

Five hundred sheets of questionnaire were distributed among students of these schools and colleges. Number of questionnaire given to students was based on the basis of their average attendance in the schools and colleges. 75 questionnaires were distributed among teachers of English of these schools and colleges. Out of these, only 50 could be collected. The Table 4.1 shows the distribution and collection of questionnaires among students and teachers.

Questionnaire

Questionnaire, given to teachers, seek their opinion regarding students' attitude towards the language and its performance level in different language skills, usefulness of materials, methods, evaluation system and parents'/guardians'/attitude towards their wards' studies. Whereas students questionnaire ask information regarding students' socio-economic and educational background, their attitude towards the language (English), teaching materials and methods.

A numerical breakdown of total number of students enrolled in different schools and colleges in different faculties and number of students opting English and their average attendance in regular classes are shown in Tables 4.2a, 4.2b and 4.2c.

Table 4.1: Distribution of Questionnaire

S. No.	*Name of Institution*	*Teachers*		*Students*	
		Distributed	*Received*	*Distributed*	*Received*
1.	C.M. College*	17	9	60	40
2.	C.M. Science College*	3	2	60	54
3.	M.R.M. College*	5	3	60	40
4.	Marwari College	5	5	60	35
5.	Millat College*	3	3	60	36
6.	K.S. College	5	3	60	30
7.	M.L.S.M. College	4	3	30	14
8.	M.K. College	2	1	30	07
9.	N.J.M. College	4	3	60	35
10.	L.C. College	3	2	15	07
11.	Zila School	5	2	-	-
12.	Raj School	5	5	-	-
13.	Marwari School	4	1	5	2
14.	L.R. Girls School	1	-	-	-
15.	M.L. Academy	4	4	-	-
16.	P.G. Department*	5	4	-	-
Total		75	50	500	300
Percentage			66.6		60

Note : *Postgraduate teaching departments, senior teachers do not engage intermediate classes regularly.

Table 4.2a: Enrolment of Students opting for English in Colleges

Sl. No.	*Names of Colleges*	*Faculty*	*No. of students enrolled*	*No. of students opting English*	*Average attendance of students in classes*
1.	C.M. College	Science	—	—	—
		Arts	577	206	25 per cent
		Commerce	327	222	40 per cent
2.	C.M. Science College*	Science	512	512	Above 50 per cent
		Arts	—	—	—
		Commerce	—	—	—
3.	M.R.M. College	Science	193	182	Above 50 per cent
		Arts	304	125	30 per cent
		Commerce	—	—	—
4.	Marwari College*	Science	300	300	
		Arts	450	250	25 per cent to 30 per cent
		Commerce	112	50	
5.	Millat College	Science	231	200	50 per cent
		Arts	75	32	Below 10 per cent
		Commerce	—	—	—
6.	K.S. College	Science	800	639	50 per cent
		Arts	295	137	25 per cent
		Commerce	90	41	40 per cent
7.	M.L.S.M. College	Science	449	363	
		Arts	157	42	Below 10 per cent
		Commerce	58	19	
8.	M.K. College*	Science	125	125	
		Arts	400	22	Below 10 per cent
		Commerce	—	—	—
9.	N.J.M. College	Science	150	138	
		Arts	242	64	25 per cent to 30 per cent
		Commerce	—	—	—
10.	L.C. College	Science	175	21	
		Arts	251	35	Below 5 per cent
		Commerce	15	10	
Total			6289	3735	1197
Percentage				59	32.04

Note : *In these institutions English is compulsory for science students.

Table 4.2b: Enrolment of Students opting for English in Schools

Sl. No.	*Name of Schools*	*Faculty*	*Total no. of students enrolled*	*No. of students opting English*	*Students attendance*
1.	Raj School	Science	-	-	-
		Arts	2	-	-
		Commerce	2	-	-
2.	Marwari School	Science	5	2	
		Arts	-	-	-
		Commerce	-	-	-
3.	L.R. Girls School	Science	-	-	-
		Arts	2	-	-
		Commerce	-	-	-
4.	Zila School	Science	-	-	-
		Arts	-	-	-
		Commerce	-	-	-
5.	M.L. Academy	Science	-	-	-
		Arts	-	-	-
		Commerce	-	-	-
	Total		11	2	-

Table 4.2c: Faculty-wise Distribution of Students studying English in Schools and Colleges

Sl. No.	*Faculty*	*Total number of students enrolled*	*Students opting English*	*Percentage*
1.	Science	2915	2272	77.9
2.	Arts	2751	913	3.01
3.	Commerce	602	342	56.08

Questionnaire of students gather following information:

(i) Student's social, economic and educational background.

Table 4.3: Mother Tongue of the Respondents

Sl. No.	*Mother Tongue*	*Frequency*	*Percentage*
1.	Hindi	142	47.3
2.	Maithili	102	34.0
3.	Urdu	46	15.3
4.	Other	10	3.3

Table 4.3 shows students' mother tongue and the dominant language used for mother tongue.

Table 4.4: Occupation of the Respondents' Fathers/Guardians

Sl. No.	*Occupation type*	*Frequency*	*Percentage*
1.	Service	160	53.3
2.	Business	74	24.6
3.	Agriculture	66	22.0
4.	Trade	—	—

Table 4.4 respondents' economic background in terms of their fathers' occupation. 53.3 per cent of respondents' background is of service class whereas 24.6 per cent belong to business class and 22 per cent have agriculture as their occupation. Not a single candidate belong to trade.

Table 4.5: Marks Obtained in English at S.S.E. Board Examination

Sl. No.	*Categories of Marks obtained*	*Frequency*	*Percentage*
1.	Less than 45	9	3
2.	45 – 50	21	7
3.	50 – 60	38	12.6
4.	60 – 70	48	16
5.	70 – 80	24	8
6.	More than 80	160	53.3

Table 4.5 shows their marks scored in English in S.S.E. Board examination. 3 per cent students got less than 45, whereas 53.3 per cent students got more than 80. Rest of them scored between 45 to 80.

Table 4.6: Medium of Instruction for Subjects other than English

S. No.	*Medium*	*Frequency*	*Percentage*
1.	Hindi	106	35.3
2.	English	194	64.6
3.	Other	—	—

Table 4.6 presents students' preference of medium of instruction for subjects other than English. 35.3 per cent of students have Hindi as their medium of instruction, whereas 64.6 per cent of students opt English as their medium of instruction. 0 per cent of respondents have other languages for their medium of instruction. This apparent inflation is largely due to the mistaken notion of science students that the medium of instruction is English because technical terms, definitions and other technical details are taught in English. But the framework of the lecture is in the locale language.

Students' Attitude

To show students' attitude towards English following tables are devised. These tables show their preference of language regarding use of English in domain of daily contact. They also show their choice of language in different situations.

Table 4.7 shows that 62 per cent of students use English in domain of education only. Whereas 24.6 per cent use it with friends, 3.3 per cent in family and 10 per cent in transaction.

Table 4.7: Use of English in Domains

Sl. No.	*Domains*	*Frequency*	*Percentage*
1.	Family	10	3.3
2.	Friends	74	24.6
3.	Education	186	62
4.	Transaction	30	10

It is obvious by Table 4.8 that 56 per cent students use English for educational purpose only. For reading and listening for pleasure 72.6 per cent prefer Hindi to English.

Table 4.8: Use English for Educational Purpose

Sl. No.	*Functions*	*Hindi*	*English*	*Maithili*	*Any other*
1.	Reading newspapers	192	108	—	—
2.	Reading magazines	176	104	20	—
3.	Listening to broadcast and watching T.V.	218	82	—	—
4.	Reading books and journals for educational purpose	132	168	—	—

Regarding their aim for learning the language their response show following preference:

Table 4.9 makes it clear that their option of English for occupational need is 34.6 per cent, for educational need 58 per cent. Whereas 1.3 per cent students study English for reference skill, 2 per cent for note taking and 4 per cent for note making.

Table 4.9: Aim of Learning English

Sl. No.	*Purpose*	*Frequency*	*Percentage*
1.	Reference skill	4	1.3
2.	Occupational need	104	34.6
3.	Educational need	174	58
4.	Note taking	6	2
5.	Note making	12	4

Table 4.10: Liking of Reading Materials for their Course

Sl. No.	*Reading materials*	*Frequency*	*Percentage*
1.	Literature	128	42.6
2.	Writing of commercial/scientific/current topics	100	33.3
3.	Reports on policies	20	6.6
4.	Topics of general interest	52	17.3

Table 4.10 shows their attitude towards reading materials. It shows that their liking is now changing. Only 42.6 per cent want literature in their course materials, 33.3 per cent like to include writings of commercial/scientific/current topics as their course materials. 6.6 per cent feel reports on politics should be included in their course material. But 17.3 per cent have view that topics of general interest should be included in course materials.

Table 4.11 shows the area of greatest difficulty. It is found that 79.3 per cent feel difficulty in spoken skill. Whereas 7.3 per cent in understanding class lectures, 6 per cent in writing answers in the examinations. Rest 6.6 per cent have difficulty in taking notes of lectures in classroom.

Table 4.11: Area of Difficulty

Sl. No.	*Area of difficulty*	*Frequency*	*Percentage*
1.	Spoken English	238	79.3
2.	Reading texts	2	0.6
3.	Understanding class lectures	22	7.3
4.	Taking notes of lecture in the class	20	6.6
5.	Writing answers in the examinations	18	6

Their opinion regarding teaching techniques and home assignment are presented in Table 4.12:

Table 4.12: Use of Hindi/English in following Classroom Situations

Sl. No.	*Situations*	*Yes*	*No*
1.	(Comprehensioning) when use of English as medium of explanation of content	198 (66 per cent)	102 (34 per cent)
2.	Use of English in explaining meanings of words and sentences	39.4 per cent	60.6 per cent
3.	Classroom become interesting when Hindi is used	202 (67.3 per cent)	98 (32.0 per cent)

Table 4.12 shows that 67.3 per cent students prefer use of mother tongue in the class, whereas English is preferred as medium for explaining contents, words and sentences by 66 per cent and 39.4 per cent of students respectively.

Table 4.13 shows students' ability in performing four basic skills. It is found that 60.6 per cent students claim that they read prescribed materials without any help, whereas 36 per cent need help. Regarding doing home assignments and exercise materials 42 per cent need help and 58 per cent do these by themselves. 66 per cent of students do not have any difficulty in understanding class lectures given in English but 34 per cent feel Hindi should be used occasionally. 65 per cent of students feel they have problem in speaking English.

Table 4.13: Performance Level in Four Basic Skills, on the Basis of Data of Students' Responses

Sl. No.		*By himself/herself*	*Take help/prepared material*
1.	Read prescribed material	182 (60.6 per cent)	108 (36 per cent)
2.	Do exercise materials in the text book	174 (58 per cent)	126 (42 per cent)
3.	Prepare notes	232 (77.3 per cent)	68 (22.6 per cent)
4.	Understand what is taught in English	198 (66 per cent)	102 (34 per cent)
5.	Expressing in class	105 (35 per cent)	195 (65 per cent)

Teachers' Opinion

Teachers' opinions were sought on students' performance level, their workload with regard to intermediate classes, teaching materials and aids, teaching devices used in the classroom, syllabus, evaluation system and guardians' attitude towards their wards.

Proficiency Level of Learners

Table 4.14 presents their opinion regarding the learners' proficiency level in the area concerned. It shows that 40 per cent teachers think that their students' participation in the class is moderate whereas 50 per cent think they (students) do not participate activity. Regarding comprehension skill, 24 per cent feel that lecture delivered is properly understood by them, whereas 54 per cent teachers think that students' understanding of the language in formal talk and out of classroom situation is only moderate.

As for spoken skill, 46 per cent think they are moderately well in formal class discussions but in response to question they are again moderate (48 per cent) while in talking among themselves they are not very well (58 per cent).

Table 4.14: Students' Participation (in teachers' opinion) in Classroom Activities

S. No.	*Participation in*	*Very well*	*Moderately well*	*Not very well*	*Very poor*
1.	Active participation in class discussion	×	20	25	5
2.	Understanding				
	Lecture	12	27	11	
	Formal talk	14	18	18	
	Out of college	12	11	11	16
3.	Speak				
	Formal class discussion	10	23	17	
	In response to question	9	24	17	
	Talking among themselves	7	14	29	
4.	Write	21	12	17	
5.	Read and understand	9	20	21	

Regarding written skill, 47 per cent teachers hold the view that very few students can write accurately at intermediate stage. Their opinion about writing skill varies between "moderately well" to "not very well" (24 per cent to 34 per cent).

Regarding comprehension, 50 per cent teachers feel most of them are moderate and 50 per cent feel that they are not very well.

Table 4.15: Objective of General English Course

Sl. No.	*Objective of general English Course*	*Frequency*	*Percentage*
1.	To develop language skill	39	78
2.	To give a forecast of English literature	4	8
3.	Teaching English grammar	4	8
4.	Teaching English as a literature language in higher education	3	6

Objective of General English Course

From Table 4.15, it is obvious that 7 per cent teachers have view that objective of English should be the development of language skill, but

8 per cent teachers think objective should be grammar. Another 8 per cent hold the view that English should be taught as literary language and rest 8 per cent believe that objective of English is to develop a taste for literary study in higher classes.

Table 4.16: Area of Difficulty in Text

Sl. No.	*Area of difficulty in text*	*Frequency*	*Percentage*
1.	Content	6	12
2.	Vocabulary	36	72
3.	Style	10	20
4.	Grammar prescribed	5	10
5.	Cultural background	21	42

Area Difficulty and Items need Careful Teaching

Table 4.16 shows the area in which students find difficulty. 72 per cent teachers think unfamiliarity with vocabulary is the major problem.

Table 4.17: Items in the Syllabus demands Intensive Teaching

Sl. No.	*Items of English syllabus need care*	*Frequency*	*Percentage*
1.	Literary appreciation	10	20
2.	Reading comprehension	2	4
3.	Written composition/letters etc	14	28
4.	Grammar and usage	30	60
5.	Prose	1	2
6.	Poetry	3	6

As per Table 4.17, twenty per cent teachers think literary appreciation should be carefully taught, whereas 60 per cent teachers hold the view that grammar and usage should be the core of teaching. 28 per cent of them think written composition, letters etc, should be given priority. Of the remaining – 4 per cent, 2 per cent and 6 per cent of teachers favour reading comprehension, prose and poetry respectively.

5

Assessment and Observation

Introduction

In chapters 2 and 3, we have described in some detail the theoretical aspects of ELT as well as the linguistic and other socio-cultural factors which seriously affect the language learning process. In the preceding chapter the relevant data as regards the ELT situation in Darbhanga have been collected. In this chapter, the data collected through questionnaires and personal interviews would be assumed. Research in social sciences had its own limitations. To avoid confusion, we have given stress on basic information and simply methods of calculation.

As explained in chapter 3, the socio-economic conditions of the place have given some distinctive twist and use to the general problem.

Assessment

Darbhanga is an economically backward area and has a thin crest of teachers, service holders and businessmen. Most of that students hail from families which have recently switched over from agricultural to white collar jobs and businesses. Their family background is essentially agricultural. Most of our students are either first or second generation learners. Question No. 5 in students'. questionnaire is about their fathers'/guardians' occupation. We find that about 53.3 per cent of students wrote "service", whereas 24.6 per cent show their fathers' occupation being business and only 22 per cent stated 'agriculture'. But Dr. A.K. Sharma (1992) shows that students coming from agricultural background is 66.17 per cent and is much higher than service and business class which is 19.07 per cent and 14.76 per cent respectively. It appears from students' response that their guardians' occupation is part-time and most of the time they are busy with their agricultural work. Since service is supposed to be more prestigious they wrote "service" as their fathers' occupation. The other surprising fact which came to our notice is that no one mentioned 'trade' as his father's occupation. The reason may be either they could not differentiate between business and trade or due to some mistaken sense of embarrassment they did not mention it.

In Appendix C, Question No. 4 is about their mother tongue. About 47.3 per cent have Hindi as their mother tongue, whereas 34.0 per cent have mentioned Maithili as their mother tongue. 15.3 per cent have Urdu as their mother tongue and 3.3 per cent have other languages as their mother tongues. This data shows that Maithili has got second position. But actually many of the students who mention Hindi as their mother tongue are first generation speakers of Hindi. In their parent's generation Maithili was spoken in the family as the first language but a language member of non-Brahmin Maithilis speakers have started disowning their mother tongue because they equate the language with the Brahminic cultures and to record their negative feeling towards the aspiration of a section of Maithilis to have a separate state for Maithili speaking people. Economic improvement and status consciousness may have also contributed to the negation of Maithili and the status of the 'rustic' language.

With the changes in the relative range and depth of these languages, and in particular with the unstable position of English in the educational system of Bihar, there has obviously been a general decline in the standard among the students. However, in response to Question No. 11 shows that 62.6 per cent students want English as a compulsory subject, whereas 37 per cent favour its removal.

The range and depth of the use of English is shown by Table 4.7 in Chapter 4. Educational domain got the highest, 62 per cent, frequency of use whereas very few, about 3.3 per cent, use English in family. Friendship domain got second highest frequency. But in reality it is much less than shown in the table. When asked to elaborate upon the type of English in this domain, students agreed they very often used code-switching and code-mixing while using the language in this area. Only about 1 per cent use the language in family and is limited only to highly educated families.

Question No. 9 shows that their use of English in different

situations is very significant. They use English mainly for educational and occupational needs. To keep these aims in mind, 56 per cent use English for their educational needs, for newspaper reading, magazine reading and to listen to Radio and T.V. their preference of English is 36 per cent, 34 per cent and 27.3 per cent respectively. Only 6.6 per cent show their inclination towards Maithili regarding reading of magazines. Perhaps this is due to the fact that there is hardly any good newspaper and magazine published in the language.

For pleasure reading, 64 per cent prefer Hindi medium whereas 5.3 per cent speak for Maithili. Only 30.6 per cent opt for English. As far as reading textbooks is concerned, 51.6 per cent want Hindi to be used as medium and 48.6 per cent prefer English.

Answer to question No. 10 on students motivation shows that 58 per cent prefer English for educational purpose whereas 34.6 per cent need it for occupational need. Only for note taking, note making and referential purpose 2 per cent, 4 per cent and 1 per cent students use English. This fact also becomes obvious from the data given in Table 4.2a, Chapter 4. The difference between the total number of students enrolled for intermediate course and number of students enrolled for intermediate course and number of students opting for English show a positive tendency towards English. It is about 59.2 per cent of total number of students. When we analyse their tendency faculty-wise (Table 4.2c), we find science students show highest positive attitude towards the language (about 77.9 per cent), whereas only 3.01 per cent arts students show interest in English, 56.08 per cent of commerce students learn English. Science students know that for further studies they need the language more than Rastrabhasha Hindi. Only competitive minded arts students opt for it.

When asked about their aim of learning, 58 per cent of them have educational need and 34.6 per cent students' aim is occupational. It is clear from this response that about 92 per cent have clear cut view about the use of English. But question regarding the suitable material for their need shows that their views are not clear. 42.6 per cent of them think literature should be continued, but 33.3 per cent think course material should be from commercial/scientific and current topics. 17.3 per cent think that material should include topics of general interest and only 6.6 per cent think that topics of politics should have place in the course. Their divergent views show that 56.9 per cent have clear cut view about their needs but 42.6 per cent are still confused and they think that literary pieces in the course material are useful.

Response to Question No. 9, 10 and 13 shows that they do not have much exposure to the language outside the class. There is no literary organisations here. Very few, about 13.6 per cent, are attached to cultural organisations. These organisations do not transact their business in English.

It is apparent that our students are not exposed to the use of English in real life situations. They have only exposed to books which is apparent from response to Question No. 9. Therefore their spoken language seems to be bookish. Only a handful amongst them with public school background are exceptions.

The greatest difficulty for the largest number (79.3 per cent) related to the spoken skill. Only 7.3 per cent have problem with comprehension skill, 6.6 per cent in note taking, 6 per cent with reading text and 6 per cent with writing skill.

Regarding reading skill, 64 per cent do not have any problem but 36 per cent feel problems. When working out exercises, 58 per cent do not take any help but 42 per cent need help. But when asked, teachers stated it was true that they tried but most of them needed help. Their writing skill does not correspond to the acceptable norms. They have lots of grammatical and contextual confusions which are already discussed in chapters 2 and 3. A list of items collected from language laboratory classes and answer scripts of Intermediate Examinees by the researcher shows the paradox of situation. There is a vast difference between the responses and the performance of students in written examination. The answer scripts present the common problems shared by students in Bihar, including Darbhanga.

When asked about their mode/method of preparations for examination, 77.3 per cent expressed their willingness to prepare notes by themselves. Only 22.6 per cent needed readymade notes. But interview with teachers and some photocopying centres of the town tell another story. There is hardly any student who do not run after notes. The tendency to score more marks (see question No. 35 of teachers questionnaire) makes them run after their teachers for notes. The teachers who supply readymade notes for them are in great demand.

In response to the question No. 1 in Table 4.12, 66 per cent students have answered in affirmative; to the question No. 3 (Table 4.12) 67 per cent of students find the class more interesting when there is a liberal use of Hindi/L_1 or the use of bilingualism in the English class. The apparent contradiction is largely due to the fact that most of the students feel that they understand the basic things when the lecture is in English. This is largely due to the fact that teachers give them so many examples and there are also repetitions enabling them to understand the contents but they are never at ease because they also feel that they do not understand a large part of the lecture. When L_1 is used, they become more relaxed and find the lesson interesting. Teachers engaging intermediate classes of science/arts/commerce streams, as a rule, find science students more responsive and making less demand for the use of L_1 in the English class because English is, by and large, the medium of instruction of science subjects. At least 3 major colleges gave weightage to the marks secured in English along with marks secured in science subjects at secondary level for admission to the intermediate or (+2) classes. English also has been made compulsory for science students. On the other hand, the medium of instruction of arts/commerce subjects is Hindi/L_1 and students are not at ease if the English lecture is not diluted by a liberal dose of Hindi/L_1.

But teacher's response is actually chaotic and it is very difficult to formulate it to a general proposition. Their response are so divergent that it is very hard to arrange it in any particular category. There are many reasons for it. Their responses reflect their view point on subjective basis. They answer the questions keeping in view those students who are in constant touch with these teachers. Large number of students, pressure to finish the syllabus and other non-linguistic reasons (already discussed in Chapter 2) have contributed to their chaotic response. Other reason is the type of colleges they belong to. Teachers of those colleges, where admission of students is restricted, opinion is far more positive as compared to those teachers who belong to those colleges where admission is open to all-comers. In premier colleges like C.M. College, C.M. Science College and M.R.M. College, students are admitted on marks basis. 75 per cent of students of these colleges are from urban background. Most of the students have either public school background from outside Darbhanga or from reputed schools of Darbhanga. Whereas M.L.S.M. College, L.C. College, M.K. College, N.J.M. College have most of their students from rural background, 75 per cent of them belong to the villages around Darbhanga and from the adjoining terrai region of Nepal. Therefore, students' entry level behaviour and their aim are so vastly divergent that even teachers fail to sustain their (students') interest in the classroom. Therefore, when asked about their active participation (Question No. 2 and 7) 22 per cent said their participation was very good, 42 per cent said it was quite good, whereas 36 per cent said it was not good. According to my own experience and observation as a teacher, the percentage of students' participation is very poor whether the institution is good or ordinary. Only 5 per cent to 10 per cent students are active learners in the class. Rest are passive learners. They prefer dictation of notes to oral presentation of learning material. This problem arises even in the language classes (language laboratory classes in P.G. English). They like their teacher should perform all the time. If asked to response or participate actively they took resort to yes/no responses. The written-form syndrome is so powerful that the spoken forms are rigidly resisted.

Students' participation depends upon their faculty also. Science students try to participate and attend classes. There are some non-linguistic reasons also. One important reason is medium of instruction of students. As it is obvious from Table 4.6 question No. 8 shows that our students belong to mixed class. No particular college has only students from English medium schools only.

Condition of inter-schools are very poor. Out of five schools, only three schools—Marwari School, Raj School and L.R. Girls' School have students but their number is limited to 11 only. In Marwari School, two students had opted for English whereas in Raj School and L.R. Girls' School, no student has opted for English. It is observed that in first year Inter classes, when students just enter colleges, students' response is positive but in second year even science students do not attend classes regularly. Their attendance grow thinner. Now they start going for tuition and coaching classes and ignore the subject because they have to give answer in the examination on contents, which are available in the market as pre-digested and ready for immediate use in the examination hall.

Attendance start falling when teacher try to ask questions or give them exercise. The researcher had a very bad experience in her attempt to involve her students actively in drills/exercises.

Their comprehension in lecture period is moderately well (Question 9). 54 per cent of teachers think so while 24 per cent think students' comprehension skill is very high. In informal talk, 72 per cent have expressed the view that they are not very well, while in situations out of college 76 per cent think their comprehension is not good. The reasons are both pedagogic and non-linguistic (Chapter 2).

Question No. 18, 19, 30 in teachers' questionnaire and question No. 21, 22, 24 of students questionnaire show that they comprehend well if their mother tongue or Hindi is used for explanation. Only 6 per cent teachers never use mother tongue. 94 per cent feel its need and use it for advantage.

As regards their spoken skill (Question 10) in formal class discussion 20 per cent teachers think their performance is very good whereas 46 per cent think they are moderately well and 34 per cent think they are not very well. In response to question only 18 per cent teachers think it 'very well', rest 48 per cent and 34 per cent think it 'moderately well' and 'not well' respectively. Talking among themselves they are not very well (58 per cent) and moderately well (28 per cent), very well (18 per cent).

For reading comprehension 18 per cent think very few students read with comprehension (Question 13) while 40 per cent opine they read with comprehension. Only 42 per cent have view that their reading is without comprehension.

About writing skill 66 per cent have view, few write as per acceptable norm (Question 12) while 34 per cent think their writing is not appropriate.

Regarding objective of general English (question No. 15) course, 78 per cent view that it should be for developing the language skills of the learner. Only 8 per cent think it should be teaching grammar whereas 14 per cent think it should be taught as a vehicle for higher education.

For specific area of difficulty 72 per cent feel unfamiliarity of vocabulary creates problem in comprehension and enjoyment of the material. 42 per cent feel it is cultural background which vex our learners.

Next comes style of the prescribed piece. Since they are always face-to-face with reported language, so when they find only change in the style they feel bewildered and confused. Therefore, colloquial language used in plays vex and confuse them. The contractions used make comprehension difficult. Content and grammar prescribed create less problems as compared to other areas.

For part of the syllabus demanding careful teaching (question No. 17) 66 per cent teachers, think grammar and its usage must be carefully taught, while 28 per cent insist on written English composition and letters etc. Next comes literary appreciation (20 per cent). For reading comprehension 12 per cent, 6 per cent for poetry and 2 per cent for prose, should be emphasised. On analysis it becomes obvious that maximum teachers feel general English course must cater to learners' occupational and educational needs. But it is also clear that they have a dim view of language items. They confuse it with grammar and usage. In fact, it is only one fraction of language items.

Teaching materials (question No. 24) and teaching aids used in the classroom are blackboard and text books. 70 per cent teachers use blackboard. Only one teacher uses audio aids, two use cartoons, one uses chart and two use pictures. There is no audio visual aids in these schools and colleges except C.M. College. But these audio aids are never used in the class. One teacher, who says she uses audio aid (Milat College), appears to be an exception. Responses to questions 14, 18, 19, 21, 24, 28, 30 and 31 show that they do not follow any particular accepted method. They are far more divergent in their approach. Therefore, one teacher from Milat College says she uses audio aids while there is no such aids in the college. Even her students say it is not used in the class. Use of teaching materials show that all the colleges except C.M. College have only blackboard as teaching material. Even textbooks are not brought by every student. They just listen to the content of the lesson. Therefore when teachers tell them to read the lesson they have many variations in their pronunciation (already discussed in Chapter 3). Their reading shows their unfamiliarity with the prescribed materials.

Teaching materials, used by students, is only textbook which is often spurious edition full of printing errors. Textbooks have no illustrations. Only few pictures are given in Lamb's Tales. But they are not at all attractive. Subject matter of textbooks is partly related to familiar Indian culture (discussed in Chapter 3) and environment and partly inherited from foreign culture which is altogether new and different from ours. Keeping in view these cultural assumptions 58 per cent teachers say 'yes' whereas 42 per cent say 'no' to the question.

Though topics are rich in variety (question No. 26). It includes scientific writings and sports writings as well. But it is not at all treated as functional item. Actually many of our teachers think vocabulary and grammatical (syntactical) items are only sufficient to learn the functional aspect of language. Their views become obvious from their responses. 76 per cent teachers think topics is rich in variety, while response to question No. 27, their response is 50-50.

Their responses show that they did not think over it at a deeper level. Their responses show that subject matter taken from different topics is thought to be authentic and full of variety. Whereas in real life situation when learners have to use the language for certain functions, they are unable to use these items for their need. Functional language is altogether different from descriptive language. Our students use it only for descriptive use. They are not at all taught how they have to agree or disagree to some view points, which type of syntactical patterns are used for any specific purpose, how some words have changed according to context where they are used. Even conventions, traditions courtesy prevalent in the culture of the language studies are not at all highlighted. We only tell them the theme or content of the prescribed piece, because question are on contents, story or character. There is no demand for the functional items. Only grammatical items (see Appendix B) bereft of context force students to know the meaning of words only and not their use in particular contexts. Therefore at times we find contextually inappropriate use of words and sentences in their writing (see Appendix B_2). These teaching materials are not at all relevant in teaching language skills, say 56 per cent of teachers interviewed. Those skills, which they particularly need for their occupation, are such as to give order, to enquire, to agreeing or disagreeing with someone, and such other functions, and educational such as, reference skill, library work, rapid reading, scanning skill, inquiring, etc. Therefore, syllabus is not conducive to teaching what our learners need (question No. 23), say 60 per cent of our teachers. Teachers' response to question No. 22 as regard the time they devote to teaching language items evoked widely divergent and inconsistent views. Most of them thought that explaining the meaning of the phrase or a new word was all that was expected of them in teaching language items to students. They do not feel the necessity of inviting the learners' attention to interesting sentence structures. Almost none felt the necessity of devising exercises or drills for these items for students.

When asked about written task given in class (question No. 28), 86 per cent of them said that only sometimes they gave written tasks due to the following reasons : time pressure, large number of students, their lack of motivation and others. They (78 per cent) correct and explain their mistakes occasionally; 60 per cent of teachers hold the view that these discussions are useful in Hindi-English mixed language. Use of only English is not interesting and useful to most of the students. In the response to question No. 27, teachers agree that only a small number of students do the task assigned to them.

Question Nos. 34, 35, 36 and 37 project guardians' interest in their wards. 78 per cent of teachers say only some of them consult the teacher about the progress of their wards and encourage them to study. 80 per cent of teachers are of the opinion that parents are more interested in the marks scored by their wards. They hardly try to see whether their wards' acquire proper knowledge of skills or not. They measure their wards' progress on the basis of marks scored by them in the examination. Even many institutions select trainers on the basis of marks scored. Therefore, there is a race for fetching handsome marks in the subject, by foul means or fair. This is reflected in the wide disparity between the marks scored (Table 4.5 in Chapter 4) and the actual performance level.

Examinations are held once in a year/session in most of the institutions but few colleges hold it twice in a session. There are no term examinations. If any, no credit accrues for the final grading. 90 per cent of teachers say our evaluation system evaluates or tests written skill only. Students are never tested for spoken skill or reading skill. In fact examination tests learners' memory power. It reflects how much a learner has internalised the content. But these days due to unfair means even this skill also is not evaluated. It can only evaluate how good a written note the learner can manage to obtain and how effectively he can put it on paper.

Conclusion

Observations presented in this chapter are merely illustrative of the broad range of socio-economic and pedagogic conditions prevalent in Darbhanga. Students of Darbhanga offer English mainly for utilitarian purpose and accordingly they show positive attitude towards the subject. But the ratio of total students enrolled, number of students opting for English and their average attendance present an interesting picture. Faculty wise analysis shows that out of 3735, 2915 belong to science and it is 78 per cent of the total number of students opting English. Next comes commerce students. The poorest percentage is of arts students. It is apparent that these students who are carrier conscious study English in all seriousness. It is another matter that the English they learn within the narrow confines of classroom without exposure to real life situation make their language skill weak and anaemic.

Though some students think that they want to prepare notes and exercise themselves, in reality the situation is altogether different. Insufficient teaching materials and equipments, faulty methods applied, wrong emphasis on teaching items in syllabus and evaluation system cause lack of drive in our students. Non-pedagogic conditions prevalent in the college and accepted unfair means have further worsened the situation. Since for examination purpose they are expected to be master of contents, they do not feel the necessity of attending classes. The extremely thin attendance of students goes to prove the unadequacy and uselessness of classroom teaching.

Most of our teachers, bowing to the popular demand for prepared notes and answers and the 'oral' method of delivering one-sided lectures to the students, are replaced by the 'worse' method of dictating answer to probable questions in the general class. They claim that this 'note-giving' attracts larger attendance and attractiveness of students in the class.

On the whole, what we find is that the causes of deviation from accepted norm is not one but many. All these are interrelated. Change in one effects the other variable and its result is before us. In this process both the quality and quantity of English taught and learnt undergo major changes in the contexts of culture and situation in which it is used.

6

Conclusion with Remedial Suggestions

Introduction

This chapter will summarise the degree to which the claims and theoretical approach presented in Chapter 1 have been supported by the findings in this study. Implications of this research will then be discussed and remedial measures for applied issues of language planning and the teaching of English as a second language would be formulated. Finally, possible directions for further related research will be proposed.

Summary

The basic premise of this dissertation has been that socio-cultural structure and cultural expectations cause the deteriorating condition of students residing in Darbhanga. The crucial point is that the accepted norms for usage of language vary with differences in varieties of the language arising from differences in contexts of culture and situations and from contact with other language in each fellowship's linguistic repertoire.

Within the socio-linguistic region of Darbhanga, several important aspects of nativisation are clearly illustrated. First, the degrees and types of nativisation of English vary directly with the relative range and depth of the use of English mainly for occupational and educational needs. Therefore, the motivation for learning English is instrumental. Quarrel of Hindi with regional languages provides a strong support to English. Poor study and teaching conditions, poor or negligible salary of teachers in privately managed institutions and the demand of social and family liabilities force teachers to adapt other side business or tuition which effect their classroom performance. Good teachers leave the job for better prospects. Those who remain either by choice or necessity hardly get any incentive or opportunity, for serious involvement in their profession. They are not free to employ and experimental work or new methods. Most of the colleges are commercial enterprise and teachers are not only exploited by the management, they are also treated shabbily by their own students because more often than not they are beating their luminous wings in void, as Shelly puts it in a different context. In government establishments conditions are still worse. Only those teachers who cater to the popular demand have some following among the students. Those who want students to work seriously often found their classes avoided and empty.

There is a total lack of equipments and trained teachers. Majority of students have very little opportunity to converse, or to listen in the language except in the class in a set (lecture) frame. Students' family background, economic condition and degree of motivation all play important part in the learning of language. The degree and types of deviations of English vary directly with the relative range and depth of English and other languages in the linguistic repertoires of English-using speech-fellowships.

Thirdly, poor learning of these students is manifestation of different constraints, linguistic and non-linguistic sprang up from the social structure. Difficulties in communication do not necessarily disappear as learner gains control of basic English grammar and vocabulary (Gumperz *et al.,* 1979). Unintelligibility is not only due to stress pattern but in their assumptions about the situation or appropriate behaviour and intentions within it. They differ systematically in their way of giving information, in structuring an argument, in their way of speaking, *viz.*, the use of different set of linguistic conventions (such as pitch, tone of voice, etc.) to give emphasis, to signal connections and changes in the focus of the argument. The difference of experience of culture, social set-up and knowledge of social norms and customs. This aspect of language is neither taught in the classes nor highlighted. Therefore, our learners are ignorant of this important aspect of language. And it is very difficult for them to think beyond their grammatical accuracy. Since they never listen or are exposed to spoken English they think grammatical accuracy is all that matters for successful communications.

Lack of proper planning and emphasis on language skills, teacher's inadequate knowledge of syllabus and recent trends in teaching methodology all resulted in poor performance by our learners. The type of examinations and its emphasis on descriptive language and contextless application of grammatical items also cause such chaotic situation. Parents' indifferent attitude to learning and their attitude to manage higher marks, by foul means or fair, for their wards, irrespective of their performance, has contributed to the degeneration of the system.

The other contributory factors affecting learning are frequent strike by teachers, 3 major strikes in about 3 months duration each in the last five years, two major strikes by non-teachers of 60 days duration, frequent bycotts and *satyagrah* by student bodies have played havoc with the academic calendar. Sessions are extended, examinations delayed for more than three years in some cases. And then suddenly there is a hue and cry everywhere to regularise the session. So unceremoniously sessions are curtailed, syllabus truncated, model questions supplied and the ritual of examination is completed. These factors have seriously affected the teaching/ learning environment in schools and colleges because hardly any attention is paid to the fulfilment of academic obligations.

In Darbhanga most of our students get less exposure to the language in real life situations. There is no literary or cultural organisations which provide exposure to the language outside the classroom. The geographical situation and economic backwardness of the place do not attract foreigners or visitors from other parts of the country. As a result, this place has almost negligible opportunity for use of the different registers of the language. Some people including NRIs do visit the place occasionally. But they also like to use mother tongue while on visit. Students residing in metropolis, on the other hand, are always exposed to the language. They have different programmes, organisations and pop shows. They get lots of opportunity and facility to develop the skill. They have before them appropriate models to widen the area of language use which are devised to our students.

Therefore, the competence level of our students is quite different from the learners in metropolis. What they had to follow is the model which is representative of the place with reflections of local culture and assumptions and beliefs. They have their own habits and mental outlook. Therefore, in collecting information through questionnaire and personal interviews, researcher had to face incomprehension and even suspicions. Teachers themselves, by and large, are ignorant of the changes introduced in the format of language teaching. They have their age old beliefs which they practise even these days. All these make language teaching a dull and unfruitful exercise. J.C. Nesfield still is the guiding light. They feel hurt if some younger teachers point out to the changing concept of acceptability and unacceptability in place of "right" or "wrong" in language use.

Though our syllabus is very ambitious, it does not give any clearcut instruction to teachers. Syllabus design is an academic process but in designing this, non-academic factors often come into play. It points out to the objectives but little or no attention is paid towards attainment of the objectives. The syllabus is designed by the board of university consisting mostly of very senior teachers of the faculty. Opinions of teachers who actually teach the inter standard students are seldom sought. Most of the teachers are, therefore, left in the dark about the purpose for which the syllabus is framed.

Textbooks are manifestations of syllabus. But there is no co-ordination between the two. There are many flaws in the textbooks, which we have discussed earlier in Chapter 2. They hardly cater to occupational needs. The old pattern written examination system often defeats the very purpose of the syllabus.

We find after the survey work (Chapters 4 and 5) that there is an obvious change in the need or aim of learners. Now their aim is occupational and developmental. They offer English for these reasons. Therefore, the emphasis should be changed from literature to language teaching. For that the whole system needs change. It does not mean that the old system of examination is thoroughly useless, but teaching of English now needs a radical change, right from planning to evaluation, to make ELT a functional and productive exercise. The indifference and apathy of students reflected in very poor attendance in classrooms must be reversed.

Implication for Applied Linguistics

Applications of linguistics for which the findings in this study are relevant include language planning and the teaching of English to non-native speakers.

Language Planning

For several decades, it has been widely assumed that linguistic and socio-linguistic theory can be applied to assist multilingual nations in the allocation of status and function to their various languages and in the standardisation of linguistic features in each of these languages used. Tauli (1977:252) observes:

> "Although language is more resistant to change than some other social phenomena, it is nevertheless subject to deliberate change and direction, even to radical change (p. 248) .... Language planning is the methodical activity of regulating and improving existing languages of creating new common regional, national, or international languages".

The outcome of language planning in Bihar casts serious doubts on the feasibility of such attempts to regulate language development and use. With regard to language status-planning, Bihar has experienced little difficulty in promoting the use of Hindi as national and official language. English is maintained as an auxiliary language. But in popular mind English has still a strong hold as a prestigious language. Too much emphasis on the languages, it is feared, may lead to detrimental effects of deculturalisation of producing 'anaemic, uprooted floating citizens .... The range and depth of English use are still growing, especially in formal contexts in which the language policy has never intended English to be used. Multilingual settings require firm language policies in order to coordinate the vital activities of government, law, commerce and education. English should not be made compulsory. Only those people study it who have to use it for their present and future needs. It is necessary to accept one's own capacity and need they offer any language. However, if such policies are to be socially realistic, they must be extremely flexible in order to accommodate the social, cultural and political variables that affect actual language use.

Teaching English as a Non-native Language

This study has gone into the important implications of teaching of English to non-native speakers, especially with regard to the analysis of divergences from native speakers norms and attitudes towards non-native variety of English.

The deviations in highly educated people are according to the functions of their language use. Hence the use of nativised features is closely related to their functions and is governed by complex sociolinguistic rules that are part of communicative competence in non-native English using speech fellowships. But in this study this does not happen. Here the deviations or unacceptable forms are due to the unawareness of the features of English. Even it is not acceptable in IE and cause unintelligibility. Our students show positive attitude towards the language but in spite of it their languages show lots of confusions and misconceptions. Their confusions and misconceptions have important consequences for the objectives and design of general English course curriculum in this study.

Communicative competence in English in Mithila is decidedly different from its native speakers. As a result, the use of texts, curricula and even teaching methodologies, designed by educators, may be inappropriate in Mithila. The main objective of English teaching in these settings is to fetch a good job for them. So the whole set-up should be directed towards it, satisfying the needs of learners.

Suggestions for Remedial Measures

(1) From the survey it is found that intermediate classes are allotted to younger teachers, while more experienced teachers are allotted degree classes and post-graduate classes. Since they are more familiar with the problems and mind-set of students, I would like to propose that intermediate classes should be given to them. Since young teachers are in learning stage and they are not well equipped with the teaching methodology and pedagogic skill. It would be fatal for our students to learn wrong things. Since these students are raw, young and full of enthusiasm, senior teacher would be able to handle them more successfully.

(2) English must be treated as a full subject. A concrete planning regarding its position must be taken.

(3) Syllabus should be cast in such a manner that its orientation should be instrumental. It must be skill oriented. If it will not cater to the needs of the student, it will always get ignored.

(4) Teachers themselves must be exposed to new advances in methods and teaching aids. The refresher and reorientation courses offered by the UGC must be fully utilised for raising the standards of teaching. These courses are now restricted to teachers of 'constituent colleges' only in our state, denying the opportunity to teachers working in "affiliated colleges". This discrimination must be removed.

(5) Teachers must be made aware of new methods, materials and the psychology of students. Their approach must be humanistic rather than mechanistic.

(6) Points of emphasis in tests and examinations should be changed. It should be shifted from knowledge of content to proficiency in skills. Class lectures must be supplemented by group discussion, debate, seminar and other methods of developing speech skills. Students should also be encouraged to participate actively in the general lectures. It may prove useful if the last 15 or 20 minutes in a general lecture period are turned into question-answer session on the topic and language items taught in that period.

(7) Examination should test learner's ability to perform certain work instead of only literary appreciation and explanations of passage.

(8) In libraries, along with reference books on some authors, books, presenting model of functional skills, should be included. Retold novels and popular magazines and books presenting certain skills (advertisement, official letter writing, script writing, etc.) should be included.

(9) Classes and their examinations must be made regular and strictly on schedule to hold the interest of the learners to the course materials and other academic activities.

(10) There should be regular interaction between teachers and guardians, also on the model of such meetings organised in public schools. They should also be educated about the actual needs of their wards, discouraging their wards to go hunting for notes and answers to expected questions provided by the professionals.

(11) Materials should be improved and the subject matter of the course material must be from familiar context. If items belonging to foreign culture have got to be introduced, the

objective must be clearly stated. Special care should be taken in writing these materials.

(12) Teaching spoken English, its cultural differences, customs, norms must be highlighted. This is the area where our learners very often fail to comprehend. They equate the English language with their mother tongue or L_1. Besides these, there are some other factors which make their speech unintelligible, it must be cared. They are:
  (i) Slow tempo of speech,
  (ii) Phrasal pause,
  (iii) Word stress,
  (iv) Some vowels,
  (v) Some consonants.

(13) Most of the colleges have discontinued with tutorial classes due to:
  (i) Shortage of teachers,
  (ii) Paucity of space,
  (iii) Very poor attendance of students in tutorial classes,
  (iv) Teacher's attitude to treat this period most casually.

This has seriously affected language teaching because effective language teaching cannot be done in a large class, often more than 150 students. The most serious casualty is the speech skill of the learners. There is no scope for students' active participation in the general lecture because most of the teachers discourage interruption in their lectures. Our survey shows that attendance in general lecture is generally very poor. General lectures for ELT should be dropped and it should be replaced by tutorial classes of not more than 15 students. Tutorial groups should be formed on the basis of the competence level of students. Thus students with high competence level should be put in separate groups.

(14) If a task is successfully accomplished by the students, it requires involvement and support from both sides. Suitable encouragement is necessary in order to conduct a good conversations. A learner could be encouraged by the use of such expressions like 'really', 'how interesting'. But only such words are not sufficient. A teacher have to accomplish it by his behaviour also.

Scope of Further Research

As discussed in Chapter 3, when languages came into extended contact, each can influence the linguistic features of the other. In the light of these features, some areas of potential research in the future are suggested below:

(1) Mechanism of linguistic changes in context with Maithili and English.
(2) Nature of linguistic variability and accounting for these variables in terms of English and Maithili.
(3) A co-relation between social setting and linguistic variables in Maithili.
(4) A study of the effect and relative importance on cumulative effect in the acquisition of English in multilingual setting.
(5) Effect of co-curricular activities in language acquisition.
(6) Social stratification of English in Mithila.
(7) A study of relationship between language and social class.

APPENDIX A

SAMPLES OF LANGUAGE LABORATORY

Samples are taken from MA students, Batch 1991-1993, in language laboratory class. The task given is "A visit to your friend". Since they feel problem in framing sentences in spoken form, they are allowed to draft the conversation and then enact the script with the help of other students. The samples are given below:

Roll – 8	*M.T. Hindi.*		
	Mr. Ramesh	:	Hallow ! How are you, Mr. Suresh.
	Mr. Suresh	:	I am quite well.
	Mr. Ramesh	:	What are you doing at present?
	Mr. Suresh	:	I am preparing for MA Examinations
	Mr. Ramesh	:	And what are you doing? Suresh
	Mr. Suresh	:	I am preparing for P.O. Examinations for Banking.
Roll – 9	*M.T. Maithili.*		
	I	:	Hello, Mr. Mohan, "How do you do"?
	M	:	"Well".
	I	:	Have you come alone? Why not your younger brother?
	M	:	He was not at house.
	I	:	O.K.
	M	:	And How are you?
	I	:	Quite well.
	I	:	Please have your seat.
	M	:	Thank you.
	I	:	Would you like to have a cup of tea?
	M	:	No, thank you.
	I	:	Then we must go on talking.

Roll – 22 *M.T. Maithili.*

I	:	Hellow Pramod: How do you do?
P	:	I am well.
P	:	Where are you coming from?
I	:	I come from Darbhanga.
P	:	How are mother and father?
I	:	They are well.
I	:	What is your preparation for examination.
P	:	Well.

Roll – 11 *M.T. Maithili*

O ! Come, Come.
When did you return back from Bombay?
Yesterday.
How are you? And how is your studies?
That's fine.
Well you have coffee or cold drink?
No thanks.
What are you doing these days?
Nothing at all.

Roll – 3 *M.T. Hindi*

Hello Mohanjee, How are you. What are you doing these days silently. I am not seeing you from last 2 or 3 days, Is something special or general. How is your Mummy and Papa and other family members.

Roll – 24 *M.T. Hindi*

The friend	–	Hi ! Nivedita. How are you?
Nivedita	–	Oh. Hellow, when did you come here, I didn't notice you.
Friend	–	Well, you were busy with that book. I had come to seek a note from you.
Nivedita	–	O.K. I will give it to you. But, tell me, how your studies is going on.
Friend	–	O.K. it is fine.

SAMPLES OF INTERMEDIATE QUESTION AND ANSWER SCRIPTS

B_1. Question papers (Intermediate course) for last six years.
B_2. Samples (Intermediate course) for answer sheets.

B_1. L.L. English Paper – I (1988)

1. *Answer any two of the following:*

(a) How did the king finally get the answer to his question?
(b) Describe how the sacred thread ceremony of Rabindra Nath and his brother. Is it possible to understand the poetry without understanding its meaning? Illustrate.
(c) How did Gandhi Jee utilise his leisure time in London? Describe his efforts to the London Matric.
(d) What are the real obstacles to the freedom of the press? How do the press owners influence public opinion?

2. *Answer any two of the following:*

(a) What did the mother of the black boy tell him? What did the black boy tell the white boy?
(b) What gifts did the passionate shepherd propose to give to the shepherdess?
(c) Why is a married man afraid in the spring season?
(d) How would the British soldier like to be buried in case of his being killed? What would happen to the burial place?

3. *Read carefully the lines and answer the questions given : Shall I meet other wayfares at night? .... who come*

Questions:

(a) Who has written these lines?

(b) Can you say who asks the questions in the above line?
(c) Why does the questioner want to knock or call about?
(d) Is the answer to the last question very satisfying to the questioner?

4. *Tick the word or phrase you believe is nearest in meaning in 'B' to the word under 'A'*

A	*B*
(1) Supple	(a) simple, (b) not stiff, (c) watchful, (d) strong.
(2) Unambiguous	(a) complicated, (b) easily detected (c) certain, (d) effective.
(3) Immobile	(a) unchanging in expression, (b) impatient, (c) attractive, (d) not moving
(4) Precision	(a) preparation, (b) freedom, (c) accuracy, (d) skill,
(5) Enchant	(a) attract, (b) invite, (c) please, (d) charm,
(6) Luminous	(a) pale, (b) wise, (c) shining, (d) breakable,
(7) Epic	(a) strong, (b) ancient, (c) heroic, (d) immeasurable,
(8) Prodigious	(a) busy, (b) brilliant, (c) wasteful, (d) marvellous.

5. *Make sentence with any eight of the following words and phrases :*

Exile, Inheritance, Conceal, Audience, Prosperity, Hung, Ered, To take live of, To sent word, had better, In cold blood, To wait upon, To have it out.

6. *Describe some of the naughty deeds of puck or, Tell the story character of either Lady Macbeth or Miranda. Or, Tell the story of David and Goliath. Or, Bring out the moral of the story, The Hidden Servants.*

7. *Sketch the character of Rana Pratap Singh Or, Write the story of "If either you".*

Paper – I (1989)

1. *Answer any two of the following:*

(a) *write a summary of Nehru' message to the youth of India. (b) How does A.G. Gardiner develop the idea that good manners are also infectious? (c) What impression of a boy's nature do you gain from reading 'My Father'? (d) Explain in your own words the meaning of freedom of the press?*

2. *Answer any two of the following:*

(a) *Show your acquaintance with "The shoulder". (b) Discuss the idea contained in "My Native Land". (c) Show your acquaintance with the poem "Uphill" (d) Briefly describe the ideas contained in "Fairy Lord".*

3. *Read the following lines carefully and answer the questions given below:*

Upon the moon I fixed my eye ... ... and nearer still:

(a) Give the title of the poem and name the poet.
(b) Where was the poet going and why were the paths dear to him?
(c) Describe the feeling of the poet as he looked at Lucy's cottage against the background of the sinking moon.

4. *Match the words in 'A' with their meaning in 'B'*

(i) Messenger	(a) Bits and pieces
(ii) Bodyguard	(b) Without any aim
(iii) Adjust	(c) Covered with blood
(iv) Fragments	(d) To wander
(v) Random	(e) Blossoming

(vi) Glory (f) Make suitable
(vii) Roam (g) A person carrying a piece of news
(viii) Budding (h) Group of men guarding an important person

5. *Make sentences with any eight of the following words :*

curiosity, twinkling, cultivate, seize, elementary, cowardice, scholar, legend, genius, autobiography.

6. *Attempt any one of the following:*

(a) Sketch the character of prosper or puck.
(b) Narrate briefly the story of "The Merchant of Venice".
(c) Describe the character you like most in "Tales Old and New.

7. *Which one act play in your selections do you like most? Give reasons for your answer. Or, sketch the character of Gerrard or Uncle Henry or, Queen Victoria.*

Paper – I (1990)

1. *Answer any two of the following:*

(a) Rewrite in brief the story of the three questions.
(b) Do you think that A Mad Tea Party is an apt title for the essay prescribed for you? Give reasons.
(c) Describe Gandhiji's life in London.
(d) Why is the sun said to be dying? What effect will this have on the earth?

2. *Answer any two of the following:*

(a) How did the Light Brigade attack the enemy?
(b) What promises did the passionate shepherd make to his love?
(c) Show your acquaintance with either A Slumber did my spirit seal or, the Little Black Boy.
(d) What is a sonnet? Summarise one of the sonnets prescribed for you.

3. *Read the following lines carefully and answer the questions given below:*

   I bring fresh showers for the thirsting flowers .... And laugh as I pass in thunder.

   (a) Give the title of the poem and name the poet.

   (b) Describe the activities of the cloud in the first four lines.

   (c) Explain the lines "I wield the flail of lashing hail. And whiten the green plains under".

4. *Match the words in Column 'A' with meaning in Column 'B':*

(i) Hermit	(a) Enigma
(ii) Riddle	(b) An outer garment
(iii) Gabardine	(c) A digging tool
(iv) Spade	(d) A large crow
(v) Raven	(e) To annoy
(vi) Pester	(f) Very small
(vii) Minute	(g) Full of sound
(viii) Sonorous	(h) Recluse.

5. *Make sentences with any eight of the following words :*

   Legend, Property, Indignantly, civility, laceration, punctiliousness, thought, opportunity, meditation, verse, messenger, radiation.

6. *Write in brief the story of As You Like It, or, sketch the character of either Lady Macbeth or Shylock. Or, narrate the story of David and Goliath in short bringing out the moral.*

7. *Show your acquaintance with the Never Nest, or, sketch the character of either Rana Pratap or Aunt Jane.*

Paper – I (1991)

1. Answer any two of the following:

(a) What, according to Gardiner, is the value of good manners in life?
(b) How did Ranjit Singhji bring about a revolution in the game of cricket?
(c) What does Dorothy L. Sayers mean by freedom of the press? Mention two important factors that control this freedom.
(d) What is Jawaharlal Nehru's message to the youth of India?

2. Answer any two of the following:

(a) Show your acquaintance with "Mr. Lear".
(b) What is an Ode? Bring out the main ideas contained in 'Ode on Solitude.
(c) What kind of freedom does Tagore want for his country?
(d) Sum up Wilfred Owen's feelings for the doomed youth.

3. Read the following lines carefully and answer the questions given here under:

Lives of great men all remind us .... seeing, shall take heart again.

(a) Give the title of the poem and name of the poet.
(b) What do we learn from the lives of great men?
(c) Use the following words in sentences so as to make their meanings clear: remind, sublime, solemn, main, forlorn.

4. Match the words in Column 'A' with their corresponding meanings in column 'B':

(i) Revenge	(a) Strong desire
(ii) Budding	(b) Something that breaks easily
(iii) Fragments	(c) Sleight-of-hand
(iv) Random	(d) Silent
(v) Mute	(e) Without any aim
(vi) Cannibal	(f) Bits and pieces
(vii) Legerdemain	(g) Retaliation
(viii) Fragile	(h) Blossoming
(ix) Infatuation	(i) Man-eater.

5. *Frame suitable sentences on any eight of the following autobiographies:*

   Curiosity, tribute, property, education, imagination, assault, battery, declamation, verse, purpose.

6. *Write in brief the story of 'Macbeth' Or, Sketch the character of either Portia or Macbeth. Or, Who was Orlando? How did he save the life of his brother? Or, Narrate briefly the story of The Nightingle, Or, Give a character-sketch of Prince Cherry.*

7. *Rewrite briefly the story of the One-Act Play 'Uncle Fire' or Who's Who, Or, Give a character-sketch of either Bhama Shah or Gerrard.*

Paper – I (1992)

1 *Answer any two of the following:*

   (a) How does Leo Tolstoy give three lessons in "Three Questions"? Explain?
   (b) What is the importance of the sun in our life? Is the sun fated to die?
   (c) What were the experiences of Tagore in the company of his father in his later days?
   (d) What prompted Gandhiji to change his ways of life in London?

2. *Answer any two of the following:*

   (a) Show your acquaintance with either "Strange fits of passion" Or "Lines Written in Early Spring".
   (b) Summarise any poem reflecting the poet's patriotic feelings.
   (c) What does the poet suggest in 'A Psalm of Life'.

3. *Read the following lines carefully and answer the questions that follow:*

A slumber did my spirit seal ……….. With rocks and stones and trees.

(a) Name the poet and the poem from which these lines are taken.
(b) Why had the poet no human fears?
(c) What does the poet mean by 'No motion has she now no force'.

Paper – I (1993)

1. *Read the passage given below and answer the questions that follow:*

   Happy the man whose wish and care ……… Whose trees in summer yield him shade in winter fire.

   (a) Name the poet and the title of the poem.
   (b) What is the poet's concept of happiness?
   (c) What does the poet mean by paternal acres?

2. *Summarise any one of the following poems:*

   (a) The Psalm of Life
   (b) A Slumber did my Spirit Seal

3. *Give a description of The Beggar Maid. Or, Give an account of the soldier and his feelings in the battlefield.*

4. *Answer any two of the following questions:*

   (a) What were the three questions asked by the King? How were they answered?
   (b) Give an account of the early life of Rabindranath Tagore.
   (c) Why does Lewis Carroll call the party 'A Mad Tea-Party'?
   (d) What impression of Ranjitsinghji do you get from the account given by Neville Cardus?

5. *Frame sentences with any eight of the following words: unfasten; greet; hermitage; breathe; indignantly; uncomfortable; sight; mutter; alarm; concentration.*

6. *Match the words in Group A with their meanings to Group B:*

A	B
Slumber	Complain
Seal	With hatred
Contemptuously	Extremely
Dreadfully	Deep sleep
Grumble	Dose firmly
Haughty	Put in a new place
Hurl	Throw
Transplant	Proud

7. *Sketch the character of Shylock, or Write in brief what happens on A Mid-summer Night in Athens. Or, Narrate how Goliath was defeated by David?*

8. *Sketch the character of Queen Victoria, or Write about Bhama Shah and his role in saving of Mewar.*

LL English Paper – II (1993)

1. *Write an essay on any one of the following topics:*

    (a) Rising Prices
    (b) Need for Communal Harmony in India
    (c) Winter Nights
    (d) An Educational Trip
    (e) Examinations

2. *Write a letter to your friend about your experience at the polling station/booth where you went to cast your vote. Or, write an application to the Hostel Warden, asking for permission to go home for a week.*

3. *Expand, in about 100 words, the ideas contained in any one of the following:*

   (a) Unity is strength
   (b) All that glitters is not gold
   (c) Happiness shared is happiness doubled
   (d) A bad workman quarrels with his tools

4. *Read carefully the passage given below, then answer the questions that follow:*

Orpheus went on through the darkness, playing his lyre all the time. The spirits of the underworld heard his sweet music and crowd heard his sweet music and crowded round to listen to him. He passed the wicked daughters of Danaus, who had killed their husbands on their marriage night. They were being punished for this by having to fill a barrel with water. The barrel had no bottom, so they could never fill it; but if they rested for a minute they were beaten with a whip. They heard the beautitul music of Orpheus and for a while they forgot their troubles.

(a) Which musical instrument did Orpheus play?
(b) What crime had the daughters of Danaus committed?
(c) How were they punished?
(d) What effect did the music of Orpheus have on them?

5. *Fill in the blanks with suitable articles:*

(a) He is .... European.
(b) .... Greeks believed in many gods.
(c) This is .... unique opportunity.
(d) He always goes for ....best.

6. *Fill in the blanks with suitable prepositions:*

(a) He did .... choler.
(b) This is the poem I was referring ....
(c) What are you talking..............
(d) The train is running .... time.

7. *Change any four of the following into passive voice:*

   (a) Advertise the post.
   (b) He gave me a present.
   (c) Where did they find the boy?
   (d) Someone has picked my pocket.
   (e) They will show her a picture.

8. *Change any four of the following into interrogative sentences:*

   (a) They are going to school.
   (b) He can work wonders.
   (c) You would know him if you saw him.
   (d) None had spoken to her before.

9. *Use any four of the following phrases in sentences of your own—*

   Ask, for, back out, come round, look into, look after.

10. *Change the following into indirect form of narration:*

    (a) Mohar said, "I want to become a doctor".
    (b) He said, "I have taken it".
    (c) The teacher said, "The sun rises in the east".
    (d) "Get your coat, Tom," his mother shouted.

11. *Correct any six of the following:*

    (a) I have come here yesterday.
    (b) He entered into the room.
    (c) I am comparatively better today.
    (d) Let us discuss about it.
    (e) He was accused for lying.
    (f) He spoke a lie.
    (g) China is in the north of India.
    (h) He is a best friend of mine.

12. *Combine the following sentences into one:*

He will win the election. This is certain.
He is highly popular among the electorates.

13. *Supply the correct forms of the verbs given in brackets:*

(a) you (go) to see a film last night?
(b) How many books on the subject you (read) before?
(c) He (write) a book on the poetry of Tagore.
(d) The delegation (meet) the Vice-Chancellor tomorrow.

14. *Punctuate the following using capital letters where necessary:*

good gracious said the captain you ought to keep a cat in your palace to kill all the rats and mice a cat said the king what's that is it a new kind of lion.

15. *Fill in the blanks with suitable verbs given in brackets:*

(a) Neither he nor I .... willing to go. (am, is)
(b) The jury .... divided. (was, were)
(c) A boy and a girl .... singing. (was, were)
(d) A hundred rupees .... a lot of money. (is, are)

16. *Translate into English:*

पुस्तकालय मनुष्य का एक बहुत बड़ा मित्र होता है जो सुख दुख में काम देता है। दुख में यह हमें सान्त्वना देता है। मन के थके रहने पर या एकान्त में रहने पर यह मन बहलाता है। यह विपत्ति में धैर्य, सुख में क्षमा एवं नम्रता, युद्ध में विक्रम और कर्त्तव्य पालन में दृढ़ता लाता है। यह हृदय को शान्ति का पाठ पढ़ाता है और शिष्टाचार की शिक्षा देता है।

INTERMEDIATE ANSWER SCRIPT

Random samples collected from inter examination 1993 in the process of evaluation at the C.M. College, Darbhanga evaluation centre held from 13th May to 21st May 1993.

Here are some samples of application.

1

Examination Hall
10.4.93

Respected The Hostel Warden,

Respectfull I want to draw your attention about the departure for the home. Recently I received a called from my butter to come to house very soon. Some urgent work have come at my house what kind of house work are is not know. It seems that some urgent work have come for help of my guardian and house come for help of my guardian and house fellows. I want to got to my house.

There fore I newant you to grant a week leave for the departure to my house. As you know I am a sttadent of your hostel. I request you to grant a work holiday.

Fortain I will be grateful you for ever.

Yours obedient
A.B.C.

2

To,
The Warden (Dear the hostel warden)
Juckson Hostel PU.

Sub.—Application for permission for leave

Sir,

Most humbly and respectfully I bring to your kind notice that I wanted to see my ailing father who is under treatment of a doctor in a private nursing home in New Delhi.

I therefore, request you kindly allow me leave from hostel from 2.5.93 to 8.5.93 for this. I shall every pray.

Yours affectionately
Name Dilip Kumar
Room no. 30

Dated : 10.4.93

3

To,
The hostel warder,
A.N. College. Patna.

Sub.—"Allow me to go home for a week".

Sir,

With due respect and humble submission, I have to say that I am bonafied boarder in the college hostel. It is extremely regrettable to inform you that my father has fallen seriously ill. My mother has called me through her letter to come home soon.

There is non to attend on my father except me. I have got him thoroughly checked up by a good physician in Patna. I am doing hard labour to prepare for my examination, but at this critical stage my father's treatment is preferably to my studies.

At present, I have to look after the deteriorating health of my old ailing father.

I, therefore, request you to give me permission to got home for a week.

Yours obediently
Deepak Kumar
ISc. II year

Dated 10.4.93

Sample from Translation

1. The Library is a very big friend of Human that help in happy and sorrow. It gives the refiends in lonly and Fired. It gives Paslens in a ccet in happy throw moiroy and poals the lesson of Sulsand It reaals the lesson of gaite. and teaches educati oviv be haviar

Question 4

1. The lyre musical instruments Orpheus play
2. Crime had the daughters of Danans Committed, who had killed their husbands on their marriage night.

Question 9.

The police backup the robber. He came round under the treatment of Dr. Sen. The examiner is now look into our answer papers.

Question 10

(a) His mother to idtom to get his coat
(b) Mohan said that he wanted a beg a doc tor.

Question 11

(a) I had come here yesterday
(b) He told a lion

Question 13

(a) You went to see a film last might.
(b) How many books on the subject you have read before.
(c) The Delegation will meet the vice-chancellor

Specimen of spellings:

Let	–	Lt, lost, late
Given	–	geven
Legal	–	ligal
Principal	–	princepal
Wrote	–	wrot's
Shown	–	showed
Found	–	finded
Wanted	–	wented
Cast	–	cost
Bogus	–	bogass
Vote	–	vot
Festival	–	fextival
Know	–	no
None	–	non
Said	–	sad
Will	–	well.

APPENDIX C

QUESTIONNAIRE FOR STUDENTS AND TEACHERS

1. *Name (Candidate)* :

2. *Class/Year* : *Faculty: Art/Science/Commerce*

3. *Name of Institution* :

4. *Mother tongue* : *Hindi/Maithili/Urdu/Any other*

5. *Father's occupation* : *Business/Agriculture/Service/ Trade*

6. *Medium of instruction* : *Hindi/English/Any other*

7. *Marks obtained in English : (S.S.E. Board Examination)*

8. *Use of English language in following domains:*

   (a) Family, (b) Friends, (c) Education, (d) Transactions

9. *Which language do you prefer : English/Hindi/Maithili/Any other language*

   (a) Reading Newspapers
   (b) Listening to broadcasts and TV programmes
   (c) Reading books and journals for educational purpose
   (d) Reading magazines

10. *What do you think should be the aim of studying English:*

   (a) Reference skill, (b) Note making, (c) Note taking,
   (d) Occupational needs, (e) Educational needs.

11. *Should English be compulsory subject? – Yes/No*

12. *Which language do you prefer (Hindi/English/Maithili/Any Other):*

    (a) In reading for pleasure, (b) In reading textbooks

13. *Do any one help you in your home assignment? Yes/No*

14. *Are you a member of literary club and cultural organisation? Yes/No*

15. *What kind of reading materials do you think will be useful and interesting for your course:*

    (a) Literature (poetry, drama, short stories, novel, prose pieces)
    (b) Writings/articles of commercial/scientific/current topics.
    (c) Newspaper reports on politics
    (d) Topics of general interest

16. *In which area do you face the greatest difficulty:*

    (a) Spoken English
    (b) Reading texts
    (c) Understanding class lectures
    (d) Taking notes of lecture in the class
    (d) Writing answers in the examinations

17. *Would you like to prepare answers or depend on readymade notes:*

    (a) To prepare notes by yourself
    (b) Depend on ready made notes

18. *Do you read the prescribed reading material by yourself? Yes/No*

19. *Do you work out the exercise at the end of the lesson by yourself? Yes/No*

20. *Are audio-visual teaching aids used in your college? Yes/No*

21. *Do you find your English class interesting when your teacher uses a mother tongue – Yes/No*

22. *Do you use dictionary at home? Yes/No*

    Which one – (a) Hindi-English, (b) English-English.

23. *Do you follow your teacher when he is using only English as medium of instruction? Yes/No*

24. *Do you like your teacher to give you the meaning of words and sentences in : Hindi/Maithili/English?*

Questionnaire (For Teachers)

1. *Name* :

2. *Mother tongue* :

3. *Teaching experience* :

4. *Workable knowledge of other languages*

5. *Name of the college* :

6. *How many classes assigned to you per week for inter students* :

7. *Students' active involvement in the classroom :*

    (a) Very good
    (b) Quite good
    (c) Not good
    (d) Very poor

8. *Are all the students in your class: From English medium schools/From Vernacular medium schools/From a mixed class.*

9. *How well are your students able to speak in English in the following situations:*

Situations	*Very well*	*Moderately well*	*Not very well*
(a) Formal class discussion			
(b) Talking about themselves			
(c) In response to question			

10. *How well are your students able to understand you when you speak to them in English in the following situations?*

Situations	*Very well*	*Moderately well*	*Not very well*
(a) Lecture period			
(b) Informal talk			
(c) Out of college			

11. *Whether they have understood what they are taught – Yes/No*

12. *Whether they can write accurately what they have listened to – Yes/No*

13. *Whether they can read the lesson on their own and understand it – Yes/No*

14. *If the teacher can help them in the class to learn how to improve their spoken skill – Yes/No*

15. *What should be the objective of general English course?*

    (a) Developing language skills of the learner
    (b) Developing a taste for English literature
    (c) Teaching grammar of English

16. *Which are the specific areas of difficulty in text for your students:*

    (a) Content

(b) Vocabulary
(c) Style
(d) Grammar items
(e) Cultural background

17. *Which part of the syllabus needs careful teaching:*

(a) Literary appreciation
(b) Reading comprehension
(c) English composition/letters etc.
(d) Grammar and usage
(e) Prose
(f) Poetry

18. *What do you do for your students who know the answer but cannot express themselves adequately?*

(a) To allow him to express in his mother tongue
(b) To give him guidance in mother tongue and ask him to express in English
(c) To guide him to speak directly in English

19. *How often do you use mother tongue in the classroom?*

(a) Frequently
(b) Sometimes
(c) Occasionally
(d) Never

20. *Do your students actively participate in the classroom activities? Yes/No*

21. *How much time do you devote to teach your students language items?*

22. *Are the teaching materials relevant in teaching them language skills? Yes/No*

23. *Does the syllabus is conducive to teach what they want? Yes/No*

24. *Which teaching aid do you use while teaching English:*

(a) Black board	(b) Audio aids
(c) Video aids	(d) Charts
(e) Maps	(f) Pictures
(g) Models	(h) Cartoons
(i) Flash cards	(j) Textbooks
(k) Illustrative periodicals.	

25. *Does the subject matter of textbook related to familiar Indian culture and environment? Yes/No*

26. *Are the topics rich in variety? Yes/No*

27. *Are illustrations attractive and from real life situations? Yes/No*

28. *Do you give written task in the classroom:*

    Quite often/Sometimes/Never.

29. *How many students really do the task in the class? Rough percentage.*

30. *Do you correct their mistakes and discuss the errors after correction:*

    Yes/No/Sometimes

31. *Are these follow up discussions more effective in:*

    English/Mother tongue

32. *Examinations are held:*

    Once/Twice/Thrice/Four times in one session.

33. *The evaluation system tests student's skill in:*

    Listening/Speaking/Reading/Writing

34. *Do parents encourage the students to study English? Yes/No*

35. *Are guardians more interested in:*

    (a) The marks scored
    (b) The knowledge of skills

36. *Do guardians consult the teacher about the progress of their wards? Yes/No*

Bibliography

Abercrombie, David (1963): *Problems and Principles in Language Study,* "Making Conversation", Longman Group Ltd., 1963, p. 57.

Adaskou, A.K.; Britten, D.; Fahsi, B. (1990): Design decisions on the cultural content of a Secondary English Course for Morocco. *"ELT Journal,* Vol. 44/1 January 1990, OUP.

Aitchison, Jean (1981): *Language Change : Progress or Decay,* Fontana Paperbacks.

Alam, Q.Z., (1989): "Code mixing (Urdu-English)" in papers in *Language and Linguistics.* Vol. 2, ed. U.S. Bahri, Bahri Publication, New Delhi.

Alexander, Richard (1988): "Examining the Spoken English of Students of European Business Studies" "Purpose Problems and Perspectives" *System,* Vol. 6, No.1, p. 45.

Allen, J.P.B. (1987): "Second Language Education in Canada: Current issues", *FOE,* Vol. 3, No. 1, January. 1987.

Altman, H.B. and C. Vaughan James (1979): *Foreign Languages Teaching: Meeting Individuals Needs,* Pergamon.

Anderson Anne, (1990): "Listening and learning and Quotations", in *The Radio Magazine of English Language, Life and Literature Learning,* Weekly on *BBC English,* programme 12.

Anthony, F.M. (1963): "Approach, method and technique", *English Language Teaching,* XVII, 2: 63-7.

Arlin, M. (1979): "Teacher Transitions can Disrupt Time Flow in Classrooms", *American Educational Research Journal,* 16(1), 42-56, Cited in Gangey (1981),

——, (1982) *The Art of English,* A certificate course for secondary schools (revised edition), Schofield & Sims Ltd., Huddersfield.

Aroti, MS. (1981): Mother tongue in the teaching of English at the undergraduate level in Rajasthan : An assessment and an experiment, M. Phil. Dissertation, CIEFL, Hyderabad.

Asher, J.J. & Price, B.S. (1967): "The learning strategy of the total physical responses : Some age difference, *Child Development,* 38, 1219-27.

Atkinson, David (1989): "Humanistic approach in the adult classroom: an affective reaction", *ELT,* 43/4 October. 1989.

Bajpai, Mridula and Pathak, R.S. (1989): *Papers in Language Linguistics,* Vol. 2, ed. by U.S. Bahri, Bahri Publication, New Delhi.

Bansal, R.K. (1969): *Intelligibility of Indian English,* CIEFL, Hyderabad.,

——— *The Intelligibility of Indian English,* CIEFL, Monograph No. 4, CIEFL, Hyderabad, p. 66.

Barron, A.W.J. (1961a): "The English dental fricatives in India", *Bulletin of Central Institute of English and Foreign Language,* 1:84-86.

——— (1961b) "English vowels for Indian learners", *Bulletin of Central Institute of English and Foreign Languages,* 1:77-83.

Batstone, Rob. (1988): "Teachers and course design : The case for a modular approach", *ELT* 42/3, July 1988.

Bell, A. and Hooper, J.B. (eds.) (1978): *Syllables and Segments,* North Holland Publishing Co., N.Y.

Bernstein, B.B. (1973): *Linguistic Large,* (eds.), Noel Minnis, "Language and Socialisation", Granda Publishing Ltd., The 14 linguistic lectures presented by the Institute of Contemporary Arts., London (1969-70).

Bertoldi, E.; Kollar, J. and Richard, E. (1988): "Learning how to learn English : From awareness to action", *ELT* 42/3, July, 1988.

Bhatnagar, R.P. (1976): "Language Problems of the Dis-advantaged": A critical look at the Indian Educational Practice, *JSL/Winter* 1976-77.

——— Bihar Intermediate Education Council, *Budget Estimates* 1991-92, Patna, B.E.C.

Black, J.W. *et al.* (1965): 'Speech and aural comprehension of foreign students', *Journal of Speech and Hearing Research,* Vol. 8.

Bobda, A.S. (1993): "Testing, Pronunciation" In *English Teaching Forum,* Bihar Intermediate Education Council (1992), *Budget Estimates* 1991-92, Patna, BEC.

Boorer, David (1974): *When Children Learn,* Evans Brothers Ltd.

Brook Nelson (1960): *Language and Language Learning,* "Language and talk", Harcourt Brace and World Inc., p. 23.

Brophy, J.E. and Evertson, G.M. (1976): *Learning from Teaching: A Developmental Perspective,* Allyn and Bacon, Boston.

Brumfit, C.J. (1978): 'Review of D.A. Wilkinsons National Syllabus' (*Ball Newsletter* 5, 1978), Reprinted as '*National Syllabus: A Preassessment in Problems and Principle in English Teaching* (Pergamon, 1980).

—— (1984): *Communicative Methodology in Language Teaching,* Cambridge University Press, 1984, p. 53.

Brown, Gillian (1977): *Listening to Spoken English,* London, Longman, p. 162.

—— (1990) "Cultural Values : The interpretation of discourse" *ELT,* 44/1, January. 1990.

Brown, H. Douglas (1981): "Affective Factors in Second Language Learning" in *Alatis,* James E., Altmanan, H.B. and Alatis, Perelop, M. (eds). *The Second Language Classroom,* Directions for the 1980's, Oxford University Press, pp. 113-29.

Brown, Roger and McNeill, David (1966): The "tip of the tongue", phenomenon, *Journal of Verbal Learning and Verbal Behaviour* 5, 325-37.

Bull, Shirley and Jonathan Solity (1987): *Classroom Management : Principle to Practice,* "Behavioural model", pb. Croom Helm 1987.

Canale, Michael and Merrill Swain (1980): 'Theoretical bases of communicative approaches to second language teaching and testing', *Applied Linguistics,* 1, 1, Spring: 1-47.

Candlin, C.N. (1976): 'Communicative language teaching and the debt to pragmatics' in Ramesh (ed) Georgetown University Press, pp. 237-56, *Georgetown University Monograph Series in Language Learning.*

Carroll, B.J. (1980): *Testing Communicative Performance,* Pergamon Institute of English, 1980. p. 5.

Cast, B.M.D. (1939): "The efficiency of different methods: Marking English composition", *Brit. J. Ed. Psych.* 9, 257-69.

Chaudhary, S.C. (1981): *Sociolinguistic Factors affecting the Learning of English,* M.Phil dissertation, CIEFL, Hyderabad.

—— (1989) *Some Aspects of the Phonology of Indian English,* Pb, Jayswal Press Ranchi, 1989, p. 2.

—— (1990): "Need for English in India and the Syllabus Reforms," *New Quest,* 81, May-June 1990.

—— (1992): "Towards a model for teaching spoken English", Paper presented at conference on World Englishes, University of Illinois, Urbana, U.S.A., April 1-3, 1992, p. 3.

—— (1993): "A case for teaching spoken English", *English Association Journal,* Vol. 7, Summer, 1993.

Chaudhary, S. (1993): *A New Course in Better Spoken English,* Sterling Publishers Pvt. Ltd., New Delhi.

Chomsky, Noam (1957): *Syntactic Structures,* The Hague, Mouton, p. 13, (1965), "Aspects of the Theory of Syntax", Cambridge, Mass, MIT Press.

—— (1965): *Aspects of the Theory of Syntax,* MIT Press, pp. 3-59.

Chun, J. (1975): "Selected Processes in Second language acquisition". Paper presented to the Fourth AILA Congress, Stullgart.

Clark, J.L.D. (1975): "Theoretical and technical considerations in oral proficiency testing," In Jones and Spolsky, pp. 10-28.

Cohen, A. (1977): "Successful second language speakers : a review of research literature", *Balshanut Shimusit,* The *Journal of the Israel Association for Applied Linguistic.*

Collie, Joanne & Slater, Stephen (1987): *Literature in the Language Classroom,* A resource book of ideas and activities, Cambridge University Press.

Cook, V.J. (1982): "Second language learning, A psycholinguistic perspective", in *Surveys – -I ed.* by Valerie, Kinsella, Cambridge University Press, p. 12.

—— (1983): "What would language teaching about, "*ELT Journal* : Vol. 37/3, July 1983.

Corder, S.P. (1977): 'Language continue and the inter language hypothesis'. In S.P. Corder & E. Roulet (eds.) *The nations of simplification, interlanguages and pidgins and their relation to second language pedagogy,* Geneva : Droz : Neuchatel : Universite de. Neuchatel.

Coder, S.P. (1981): *Error Analysis and Intermediate,* Oxford University Press.

Corder, S. Pit. (1978): 'Trends in EFL', *SPEA Journal,* 214, pp. 11-23.

Currie, W.B., Sturtridge, G. & Allwright, J. (1972): A technique of teaching medical English, in International Congress of Applied Linguistics, Proceedings, 3, Heidelberg, Gross.

Das, Mohajiteswar (1989): "Two ten days orientation programmes for teachers of English to tribal learners", *FOE,* Vol. 5, No. 4, October, 1989.

David, Annie (1989): "Do we understand CLT rightly", paper presented at the seminar on communication language teaching CIEFL, Aug, 1988, *FOE,* Vol. 5, No. 4, October, 1989, p. 18 13.

DeLanerolle, K. (1953): "The intonation of Sinhalese and its relevance in the initial stages of teaching of English as a second language to Sinhalese children", *Unpublished* paper, Institute of Education, London.

Devies, Alan (1968): *Language Testing Symposium,* Oxford University Press, 1968, p. 1.

—— (1982): "Language Testing I", in *Surveys I* (ed), Valerie Kinsella, Cambridge University Press, 1982.

Droff, Adrian (1988): *Teach English: A Teaching Course for Teachers,* Cambridge University Press.

Dublin, Fraida (1989): The odd couple: reading and vocabulary, *ELT,* 43/4, October, 1989.

Durant, Alen (1987): "Historical context for interest in English, *Focus on English,* Vol. 3, No. 1, January, 1987, p. 4.

Dustoor, P.E. (1954): "Missing and intrusive articles in Indian English", *Allahabad University, Studies,* 31, 1-70.

—— (1955): "Wrong, usurping and dispossessed articles in Indian English", *Allahabad University Studies,* 32, 1-17.

Edge, Julian (1990): "It works: The least we can do is write to each other", *Focus on English,* Vol. 6, No. 1, January, 1990, p. 25.

Ellis, Rod (1982): "Internal use formal approaches to examination language teaching, "*ELT Journal",* Vol. 36/2, January.

Enkvist, N.E. (1982): *Surveys I* ed. Valeri Kinsella, "Categories of situational context from the prescriptive of stylistics", Cambridge University Press, p. 65.

Ervin Tripp, S.E. (1974): Is second language learning like the first? *TESOL Quarterly,* 8.2, 111-29.

Fathman, A. (1975): "The relationship between age and second language productivity ability," *EL,* 25, 2, 245-53.

Fillmore, L.W. (1976): "Individual differences in second language acquisition", Asilomar Conference on Individual, *Difference in language ability and language behaviour.*

Fishman, J.A. (1966): *Language Loyalty in the United States,* Mouton, p. 428.

Fishman, J.A. (1968): *Reading in the Sociology of Language:* The Hague and Paris, Mouton.

—— (1972): *The Sociology of Language,* Rowley, Massi Newbury House.

Firth, J.R. (1950): 'Personality and language in society, *The Sociological Review,* 42.2, 37-52, Also in Firth 1957b.

Gardener, R.C.; Smythe, P.C.; Clement, R. & Gliksman, L. (1976): "Second Language Learning : A social psychological perspective", *Canadian Modern Language Review,* 32, 3, 198-213.

Glaser, R. (1969): Linguistics Kriterien der stibeschreibung Typescript of Habilitations schriff, Leipzig: Karl-Marks Universital, Sektion Theoretische Undangewandle Sprachwissenschaft.

Glynn, T. (1982): 'Antecedent control of behaviour in educational contexts', *Educational Psychology,* 2 (3-4), 215-29.

Goffin, R.C. (1934): "Some notes on Indian English", *S.P.E. Tract, No. 41,* Oxford: Clarendon Press, p. 31.

Gopalkrishnan, G.S. (1960): "Some observations on the South Indian Pronunciation of English", *Teaching English,* 6.2, 62-67, April, Bombay.

Gumperz, J.J. (1972): "Introduction", In J. Gumperz and D. Hymes, eds., p. 16-20.

—— and Hymes, D. (eds.) 1972: *Directions in Sociolinguistics.* The ethnography of communication, New York, etc. Holt, Rinehart and Winston.

Habermas, J. (1970): 'On systematically distorted communication' *Inquiry,* 13, 3 Autumn : 205-18; also in H.P. Dreitiel (ed) 1970, Recent sociology No. 2 patterns of communicative Behaviour, New York, Macmillan, under the title '*Towards a theory of communicative competence*'.

Hai, M.A. and W.J. Ball (1961): *The Social Structure of English and Bengali,* Dacca, University of Dacca.

Halliday, M.A.K. (1973): *Explorations in the Functions of Language,* London, Edward Arnold.

Harasawa, Masayoshi (1974): "A critical survey of English language teaching in Japan : A personal view", in *ELT,* 29/1, October, 1974.

Harold, Palmer (1964): *Principles of Language Study,* London Oxford University Press, p. 57.

Harry P. (1962): A Study of Spoken Gujarati in its Relation to the Teaching of English to Gujarati Learners, Unpublished paper. School of Applied Linguistics, University of Edinburg.

Hatch, E. (1976): "Conversational analysis an alternative methodology for second language exquisition", *Research Proceedings of the NWAVEV Conference,* Georgetown.

Heltai, Pal (1989): "Teaching vocabulary by oral translation", *ELT,* 43/4, 1989.

Hirst, Paul (1974): *Knowledge and the Curriculum,* London, Routledge and Kegan Paul.

Hirvela, Alan and Joseph Boyle (1988): 'Literature Courses and Students, Attitudes, '*ELT' Journal,* Vol. 42/3, July 1988, Oxford University Press.

Holee, Henri (1980): *Foreign Language Teaching: Meeting Individual Needs.* Chapter 3, Pergamon Institute of English, p. 35.

Hymes, D. (1964): *"Language in Culture and Society : A Reader in Linguistics and Anthropology,* New York, Harper & Row.

—— (1967): "Models of interaction of language and social setting, *Journal of Social Issues,* 33, 8-28.

—— (1971): *On Communicative Competence,* Philadelphia, University of Pennsylvania Press (extensively extracted in pride and Holmes, 1972 and Brumfit and Johnson, 1979 : 5-24, from which cited).

—— (1972): *Models of the Interaction of Language and Social Life,* In J. Gumperz and D. Hymes eds., pp. 54

—— (1977): *Foundations in Sociolinguistics: An Ethnographic Approach,* London : Tavistock.

—— (1984): "Sociolinguistics: Stability and Consolidation" *International Journal of the Sociology of Language,* 45, 39-45.

Jacob, P.G. (1987): "Cultural competence in E.S.P., Curriculum", *E.S.P.* 6/3, 1987.

Jha, Gobind (1974): *Maithili Bhasha Ka Vikash,* Sunil Printing Press, Patna.

Jakobovits, Leon A (1970): 'Prolegomena to a theory of communicative competence', in Lugton, 1970:1-39.

Johnson, Keith and Keith Morrow (1981): *Communication in the Classroom :* Application and Methods for a communicative approach, 'Principles of communicative methodology', Longman Group Ltd.

Jordon, R.R. (1990): "Pyramid discussions", *ELT,* 44/1, January, 1990.

Kachru, B.B. (1965): The "Indianness" in Indian English Word (405-8).

—— (1966): *Indian English: A Study in Contextualisation,* In E. Bazell, *et al.*, eds. In memory of J.R. Firth, London, Longman, pp. 255-87.

—— (1973): "*Towards a Lexican of Indian English*", In Braj B. Kachru *et al.*, (eds) *Issues in Linguistics : Papers in Honour of Henry and Renee Kahane,* Urbana University of Illinois Press.

— (1976): *Models of English for the Third World:* Whiteman's linguistic burden a language pragmatics, *TESOL Quarterly,* (10)2.

—— (1978): "Code-mixing as a communicative strategy in India", In James E. Alatis (ed), *International Dimensional of Bilingual Education,* Washington, D.C., Georgetown University Press (Monograph series on languages and linguistics).

—— (1981b): *The Pragmatics of Non-native Varieties of English,* In L. Smith, ed., p. 18.

—— (1981c): "Socially realistic linguistic: The Firthian tradition": *International Journal of the Sociology of Languages,* 31: 65-89.

—— (1982a): "The bilingual's linguistics repertoire", in Berverly Hartford, Albert Valdman, and Charles R. Foster, (ed) *Issues in International Bilingual Education : The Role of the Vernacular,* New York and London, Plenum Press, pp. 25-57.

——, (1982b): *Models for Non-native English,* In B. Kachru ed., pp. 3-57.

——, (1983): *The Indianisation of English,* Delhi, Oxford University Press, pp. 217-220.

Kelkar, Ashok R. (1957): 'Marathi English: A study in foreign accent", *Word,* 13:2, 268-82.

Kindersley, A.F. (1938): "Notes on the Indian idioms of English: style, syntax and vocabulary", *Transactions of the Philosophical Society,* 25-34.

Kinsella, Valerie (1978): *Language Teaching and Linguistics : Surveys,* Cambridge University Press.

Krashen, S.P. (1977): "The monitor model for adult second language performance", In M. Burt. H. Dulay & M. Finoccohario (eds.), *Viewpoints on English as a Second Language,* New York, Regents.

—— (1982): *Principles and Practice in Second Language Acquisition,* Oxford, Pergaman Press.

—— (1980): *Teaching English to Tribal Learners,* M. Phil. Dissertation, CIEFL, Hyderabad.

Kundu, M. (1982): "Teaching in a poly-cultural context: Lessons from concept, trends and developments in some relevant foundation disciplines", *Journal of Higher Education,* Vol. 8, No. 2, Autumn 1982, University Grants Commission, New Delhi.

Labov, W. (1970): "The study of language in its social context", *Studium General,* 23, 30-87, Also in Giglioli (1972), 283-308 and in Pride & Holmes (1972), 180-202.

—— (1972): "The isolation of contextual styles", In *Sociolinguistic Patterns.* Philadelphia, University of Pennsylvania Press.

Lal, B.K. (1981): *L_1 interference in the acquisition of English : An exploration of the special problems encountered by the Kondh tribal students of Orissa* in acquiring English, M. Phil. Dissertation, CIEFL, Hyderabad.

—— (1969), *Language and Society in India,* Indian Institute of Advance Study, Simla, 1969 (1st ed.).

Latchman, M. Khubchandani (1967): "Functional importance of Hindi and English in India", *Source book of Raw Data : India Yearbook* 1959, 1966, Infra Press and Advertisers Yearbook 1966, Seminar, 67, p. 14, September, 1967.

Lattey, E. (1975): "Second language acquisition: environments and strategies", In C. Molony, H. Zobl. & W. Stolting (eds.) *German in Contact with other Languages,* Monograph in linguistics and communication sciences, Kroberg, Skriptor Verlag.

Leech, G. and Svartvik, J. (1975): *A Communicative Grammar of English,* London, Longman.

Le Page, R.B. (1968): "Problems to be faced in the use of English as the medium of education in four West Indian Territories", in *Language Problems of Developing Nations,* eds. Fishman, J.A. *et al.,* pp. 431-42, John Wiley and Sons, Inc. N4.

Le Page, R. (1975): "Socio-linguistics and the problem of competence", *Language Teaching and Linguistic Abstracts,* 8, 3, July, 137-56, reprinted in Kinsella, 1978: 39-59).

Le Page and Tabouret – Keller, A. (1979): "Theoretical Aspects of, Sociolinguistics", Studies in Pidgin and Creole languages, Unpublished paper, circulated at CIEFL, Hyderabad, India.

Lewis, E.G. (1974): Linguistics and Second Language Pedagogy, *Language Testing* Mouton, 1974.

Littlewood, W.T. (1981): *Communicative Language Teaching: An Introduction,* (Great Britain: Cambridge University Press, p. viii-ix).

Llamzon, Teodora A. (1977): Emerging patterns in the English language situation in Singapore today, In W. Creux ed, pp. 34-45.

Lowenberg, Petter Harper (1984): *English in the Malay Archipelago: Nativisation and its function in a sociolinguistic area,* Ph.D. Dissertation, 1984, Urbana Illinois, pp. 2-18.

Lynch Tony (1989-1990): "Listening and learning and quotations, in the *Radio magazine of English Language, Life and Literature Learning* – weekly on BBC English, programme 12.

Manuel, Mrs. Lima (1986): *Materials for Remedial Teaching,* M. Phil. Dissertation, JNU, Delhi.

Marland, M. (1975): *The Craft of the Classroom,* Heinemann Educational Books Ltd., London, p. 84.

Martinat, A. (1962): *A Functional View of Language,* Oxford, The Clarendon Press.

Martin, J.E. (1984): *English Language (REP),* Level Elektra Educational Publishing Comp. Ltd.

Mathai, Samuel (1951): *The Position of English in India,* In Partridge and Clark, 1951, pp. 97-8.

McArthur, Tom (1983): *A Foundation Course for Language Teachers.*

McDonough, J. (1977): "English language teaching and the role of literature", *Indian Journal of Applied Linguistics,* 3/2, June 1977.

McDonough, S.H. (1981): *Psychology in Foreign Language Learning,* George Allen & Unwin Publishers Ltd.

McFarland, H.S.N. (1971): *Psychological Theory and Educational Practice,* Routledge & Kegan Paul Ltd.

McGrath, J. (1978): *Comprehensive English,* Book 1, Holems McDoughall Ltd.

Mclntire, R.W. (1974): "Guidelines for using behaviour modification in education," in R. Ulrich, T. Stachnik and J. Mabry (eds), *Control of Human Behaviour,* Behaviour Modification in Education, 3, Scott, Foresman and Co. Glenview, Illinois, p. 408-13.

McNaughton, S. (1981): "Low progress readers and teacher instructional behaviour during oral reading the risk of maintaining instructional dependence", *The Exceptional Child,* 28(3), 167-76.

McNaughton, S. and Glynn, T. (1981): "Delayed versus Immediate Attention to Oral Reading Errors : Effects on Accuracy and Self Correction", *Educational Psychology,* 1(1) 57-63.

Meek, Margaret & Miller Jane (1984): *Changing English : Essays for Harold Rosen,* Heinmann Educational Books.

Mehrotra, Raja Ram (1982): *Indian English: A Sociolinguistic Profile,* in J. Pride, ed. 150-73.

Micheau, C. & Billmyer, K. (1987): Discourse Strategies for Foreign Business Students: Preliminary Research Findings. *E.S.P.,* 6/2, 1987.

Miller, G.A. (1951): *Language and Communication,* McGraw Hill Book Co., p. 89.

Minnis, Neel (1973): *Linguistic Large :* 14 Linguistic Lectures presented by the Institute of Contemporary Arts, 1969-70, Granda Publication (1973).

Mishra, Arpita (1985): "Language in abroad : A sociolinguistic study of conversations in interethnic settings, *Indian Journal of Applied Linguistic,* Vol. 11, No. June 1985, Malinowski, B. (1935), *Coral Gardens and their Magic,* Vol. 2, London, Allen & Unwin.

Moriani, Luciano (1987): "Contradictions – Breaking the rules of coherence", in *FOE,* Vol. 3, No. 1, January, 1987, p. 35.

Mosback, Gerald (1990): "Notional Syllabus and Textbook Design on Communicative Principles – English Everyday", *FLT,* 44/1, January, 1990.

Moulton, William G. (1961): "Linguistics and Language Teaching in the United States, 1940-1960" in Mohrman, Christine, Sommer felt, Alf, and Whatmough, Joshua (Eds.), *Trends in European* and *American Linguistics,* 1930-1960 (Utrecht. Spectrum Publisher), p. 89.

Mukherjee, Ranajit (1986): *Teaching Paragraph Writing through an Experience Approach,* M.L.H. dissertation, CIEFL, Hyderabad.

Munby, John (1978): *Communicative Syllabus Design,* Cambridge University Press.

Naerssen, M.V. & Riggenbach, H. (1987): "Evaluating Oral Skills in an EST programme Native English-speaking Scientists Respond to Chinese Scientists' English *E.S.P.* 6/3, 1987.

Naidu, P.G. (1993): "One function, several ways: inviting, making and responding to suggestions", *In English Teaching Forum.*

Nair, Rama, (1989): "Workshop on Listening and Oral Skills", 4-6 January, 1989, *FOE,* Vol. 5, No. 2, April, 1989.

Nolasco, Rob, (1989): "Workshop on Listening and Oral Skills", 4-6 January, 1989, *FOE* Vol. 5, No. 2, April, 1989.

O'Connor, J.D. and G.F. Arnold (1977): *Intonation of Colloquial English* (2nd ed), London, Longman.

Palmer, H.E. (1962): *Introduction to Grammar of English Words,* Longmans, 1938/ELBS.

Palmer, Harold, E. (1964): *The Principles of Language Study,* "The student and his aim', Oxford University Press.

—— (1968): *The Scientific Study and Teaching of Language,* 'The Function of Teacher', pp. 163, The principles of linguistic pedagogy (45), Oxford University Press.

Pandit, P.S. (1964): "Indian readjustments in the English consonant system", *Indian Linguistics,* 25, 202-5.

Pass'e, H.A. (1947): "The English Language in Ceylon," Unpublished Ph.D. Dissertation, University of London.

Patnaik, B.N. (1985): 'Language teaching and discourse', *Language Forum,* 10, No. 1-4, April 1984, March 1985.

Paruchuri, Usha Prasad, (1992), Classroom Communication in English Classes of Different Sizes: An exploratory study, M.Phil dissertation, CIEFL, Hyderabad.

Pearson, Elorise (1988): "Learner strategies and learner interviews", in *ELT Journal,* Vol. 42/3, July, 1988, OUP.

Pilliner, A.E.G. (1952): "The Application of Analysis Variance to Problems of Correlation", *Brit. J. Stat. Psych.* 5, 31, 38.

Porte, Graeme (1988): Poor language learners and their strategies for dealing with new vocabulary, *ELT,* 42/3, July 1988.

Prabhu, N.S. (1982): '*The Communicational Teaching Project', South Indian:* Nimco, Madras, The British Council.

Perren, G.E. (1968): "Testing Spoken English: Some Unsolved Problems", in Davies (1968).

Pramanik, T.K. (1988): *A study of some affective variable, related to learning English as a second language at the post-secondary stage in Orissa,* Ph.D. dissertation, CIEFL, Hyderabad.

Prasher, S.V. (1979a): *Certain Aspects of the Functions and Forms of Indian English: A Sociolinguistic Study,* Ph.D. dissertation CIEFL, Hyderabad.

Prasher, S.V. (1979b): "Educated Indian Bilinguals: Attitude to English", *Indian Journal of Applied Linguistics,* Vol. 5/2, June 1979.

Prator, C.H. (1968): The British Heresy in TESL, in J. Fishman, C. Ferguson and J. Das Gupta, eds., pp. 459-76.

Pride, J.B. (1971): The social meaning of language, "Code switching", OUP, p. 26.

Pride, J.B. & Hollmes, J. (eds) (1972): *Sociolinguistics, Harmondsworth,* Penguin Books.

—— (1963): A Report on English Teaching in India (Mineographed, 1963).

Quirk, Randolph (1981): 'International Communication and the Concept of Nuclear English", In L. Smith. ed., pp. 151-65.

Ramsaran, Susan (1983): 'Poetry in the language classroom', *ELT* Journal, Vol. 37/1, January, 1983, OUP.

Ramsey, C.A. & Wright E.N. (1974): "Age and second language learning", *Journal of Social Psychology,* 94, 51-121.

Rantha, J. Ananthy (1983): '*English Used in the Classroom: A Study of Form and Function,* JNU, Delhi, M.Phil dissertation, 1983.

—— (1989): *Report of the Curriculum Development Centre in English,* CIEFL, Hyderabad, University Grants Commission, New Delhi, 1989.

Richard, J.C. (1971): "Error analysis and second language strategies", *Language Sciences,* 17, 12-22.

Rivers, Milga M. (1968): *Teaching Foreign Language Skills,* The University of Chicago Press.

Rivers, Milga M. (1983): *Communicating Naturally in L_2: Theory and Practice in a L_2*, Cambridge University Press (1st ed).

Robinson, P.J. (1989): "A rich view of lexical competence", *ELT* 43/4, October, 1989.

Sapir, Edward (1963): *Language: An Introduction to the Study of Speech,* Granda Publication.

Saraswathi, V. (1978): *Towards a Core Remedial Grammar Based on Error Analysis,* M. Litt. Dissertation, CIEFL, Hyderabad.

Satyam, E. Aruna (1986): *Psycho-social Correlates of Comprehension in the L_2 of Adolescent Bilinguals,* M.Phil. Dissertation, CIEFL, Hyderabad.

Savignon, Andra J. (1972): "Communicative competence: An experiment", in *Foreign Language Teaching,* Philadelphia, Centre for Curriculum Development.

Swahney, S.K. (1980): *Sociolinguistic factors affecting acquisition of English as second language,* M. Litt. Dissertation, CIEFL, Hyderabad.

Scovel, T. (1969): "Foreign accents, language acquisition, and cerebral dominance", *LL,* 19, 2/4, 245-53.

Selinker, L. (1972): "Inter language", *IRAL,* 10, 3, 209-31, reprinted in Richards (1974).

Shafire, William (1991): "Ins and outs of prepositions", in *Frontline,* August 17-30, 1991, National Press, Madras.

Sharma, A.K. (1992): *The Teaching and Testing of Grammar at Intermediate Level in Bihar,* Ph.D. dissertation, Bhagalpur University, Bihar.

Sen, Julu (1986): *A Proposal for an Oral Communication Component in the Plus 2 English Syllabus in West Bengal,* M.Phil. Dissertation, CIEFL, Hyderabad.

Side, Richard (1990): "Phrasa verbs: Sorting them out", *ELT* journal, Vol. 44/2, April, 1990, OUP.

Sinclair, and Coulthart, R. (1974): Forewords on Analysis of Discourse, London, OUP.

Singh, Amrik, (1984): *Asking for Trouble,* Vikas Publishing House, Pvt. Ltd., New Delhi.

Sisson, R.R. (1971): 'The description and comparison of stress in southern British English and Hindi', *Linguistic: An Introduction Review,* 17, 35-60.

Scott, Roger (1981): "Speaking" in *Communication in the Classroom* (ed) Keith Jonson and Keith Morrow, Longman Group Limited.

Sivaraman, Shanthi (1992): 'The stubborn idiom' in *Career and Competition Times, The Times of India,* Patna, August 1, 1992.

Spolsky, B. (1969): "Attitudinal aspects of second language learning", in *Language Learning,* Vol. 19.

Spolsky, Ellen (1989): "I came to bury Caesar, not praise him" teaching resisting reading, *ELT,* 43/3, July 1989.

Steiner, F. (1970): 'Performance objectives in the teaching of foreign languages', *Foreign Language Annuals,* 3/4.

Strevens, Peter (1977): *New Orientation in the Teaching of English,* London, Oxford University Press.

Strevens, P. (1977b): English as an International language : When is a local for English a suitable model for ELT purposes! *ELT Documents* (forthcoming), London: British Council.

—— (1977c): English for special purpose: An analysis and a survey: studies in language learning (forthcoming).

—— (1978): Language Teaching and Linguistics: Surveys (ed.) Valerie Kinsella, *Special Purpose Language Learning,* Cambridge University Press.

Sudhakar, G. (1987): *Structuralist grammar and communicative grammar in English classes in regional medium schools,* M.Phil. dissertation, CIEFL, Hyderabad.

Tarinayya, M. (ed.) (1992): *English Language Teaching.*

Tauli, Walter, (1977): Language Planning, In Oscar Urbevillegas, ed. *Issues in Sociolinguistics*, The Hague, Mouton.

Taylor, B., (1965): "The use of overgeneralisation and transfer learning strategies by elementary and intermediate students of ESL" LL, 25, 1, 73-107.

Taylor, Susan (1969): '*Preliminary study of the stress system in Indian English,* Division of English as a second language, University of Illinois, Urbana, Mimeographed.

Thomas, C.J. (1992): *A Comparative Study of the Spoken English of Junior Intermediate Students with Reference to Medium of Instruction:* M.Phil dissertation, CIEFL, Hyderabad.

Trim, J.L.M. (1978): "Language for Adult for Learners", *Language Teaching and Linguistics: Surveys* (ed) Valerie Kinsella, Cambridge University Press, 1978.

Trojan, F. (1952): *Der Ausdrct der Sprachstimme,* Vienna and Dusseldorf: Maudrich.

Tudom, Ian (1989): "The role of L_1 stimulus materials in L_2 communicative activities", *FOE,* July 1989.

Usmani, Mufti, A.H. (1965): '*A study of the teaching of English as a foreign language in the secondary schools of the Peshawar region',* Unpublished Ph.D. dissertation, Texas Technological College.

Vallette, Rebeconca M. (1977): *Modern Language Testing* (2nd eds.), New York, Harcourt Brace Jovanovich.

Verma, S.K. (1976): "Code switching: Hindi English", *Lingua* 38, 153-65.

Verma, S.K. (1982): *Swadeshi English: Form and Function* in *J. Pride, ed.*

Vivekananda, Swami (1957): *Education,* T.S. Avinashilingam (eds), Sri Ramkrishna Math Printing Press, Madras.

Wade, Barrie (1982): *Language Perspectives: Papers from the Educational* Review.

Weinreich, U. (1953): *Language in Contract,* Mouton.

Wheldall, K. and Merrett, F.E. (1984a): "Training Teachers to be more positive", in S. N. Bennett and C.W. Desforges (ed.) *Recent Advances in Classroom Research,* Monograph of the British Journal of Educational Psychology, Scottish Academic Press in association with the British Psychological Society, Edinburgh.

West, M. (1926): Learning to Read a Foreign Language : An Experimental Study, Longmans.

White, Cynthia (1989): "Negotiating Communicative Language Learning in a tradition setting", *ALT* 44/3, July, 1989.

Widdowson, H.G. (1971): *The Planning of the Language Teaching Operation, English Student,* Series 8, Oxford University Press, 1971.

—— (1977): The description of scientific language, *Indian Journal of Applied Linguistic,* 3/2, June 1977.

—— (1978a): *Teaching Language as Communication,* Oxford University Press.

—— (1978b): The significance of simplification, *Studies in Second Language Acquisition.*

Widdowson, H.G. (1978c): '*National Functional Syllabuses,* Part IV in Blatchford and Schachter, 1978, 33-5.

—— (1979): *Exploration in Applied Linguistics,* Oxford University Press.

—— (1983): *Learning Purpose and Language Use,* Oxford University Press.

—— (1984): *Explorations in Applied Linguistics 2,* Oxford University Press.

Wilga, M. Rivers (1968): *Teaching Foreign Language Skills,* 'Objectives and Methods', The University of Chicago Press, (1968).

Wilkinson and Bhandarkar (1984): *Methodology and Techniques of Social Research,* Himalaya Publishing House, Bombay.

Wilkins, DA. (1976): *Notional Syllabus* (1976), rep. Great, Britain, Oxford University Press, 1976.

William, T. Littlewood (1981): *Communicative Language Teaching : An Introduction,* (Great Britain, Cambridge University Press, 1981).

Wiseman, S (Ed.) (1961): *Examination and English Education,* Manchester University Press.

Wong, Irene F.H. (1983): Simplification Features in the Structure of *Colloquial Malaysian English,* in R. Noss. ed.

Yadav, Y.P. (1980): *Time, Tense and Aspects of English and Maithili: A Comparative Study,* M.Phil dissertation, CIEFL, Hyderabad.

—— (1983): *Movement Rules in Maithili and English: Their Implication for the Theory of Government and Binding,* Ph.D. dissertation, CIEFL, Hyderabad.

—— Yalden, Jenice (1983): *The Communicative Syllabus: Evaluation, Design and Implementation,* 'Context and

Function, The Roots of Change', Pergamon Institute of English (1983 ed.).

—— Yule, George (1985), *The Study of Language: An Introduction,* Cambridge University Press.

——, and Wayne Grory (1989): "Survey interviews for interactive language learning", in *ELT,* 43/2, April, 1989.

INDEX

Accuracy, 86-88, 172-73
activities, 90-91
Administrative factors, 55
Adult learning, distinctive features, 37
Aesthetic features, 68
niceties, 45
Affiliated colleges, 177
Alexander, R., 110
Analogy, 28, 38
Anthologies, 63-65
Appropriate tasks, 33
Area-centred ELT Research, 17-18
Army language course, 77
Aroti, Ms., 18
Aruna, Satyam E., 19
Assessment, 96-98, 160-65
demands, 100
Assimilation, 32
Audibility, 32
Audiolingualism, 77
Audio-visual aids, 24
Awadhi language, 21

Babu English, 115
Bad learners, 38
Bad pupil, 38
Balilect, 127-28
Bansal, R.K., 55
Basic English, 59
Basic-socio-linguistic concept, 116
Bazaar, 30, 82, 84
Bearer English, 115
Bhatnagar, R.P., 120
Bhojpuri language, 21
Bihar, educational system, 161-62
Bihar Intermediate Education Council, 149
Bilingual's mother tongue, 122
speakers, 15
Bilingualism, 121, 163
Bookish Associations, 121
British English, 82
Brumfit, C.J., 71, 79, 89, 90
Butler English, 115

Candlin, C.N., 48
Carroll, B.J., 103, 104
Change linguistic behaviour, 43
Chaudhary, S.C., 15, 18, 55, 63, 114
Chomsky, Noam, 69, 142
Choudhary, S., 147
Chun, J. 39
Classroom activities, students participation, 158
Classroom methodology, 52-53
question-answer method, 85-86
teaching, 74-75
Clue-Laden system, 90
Code-switching, 143
College teaching programmes, 22
Collocational deviation, 145
Communication, 69-75
developing phenomenon, 73
forms, 75
socio-linguistic features of, 108
Communication needs, identification of, 71
Communication Needs Processor, 46, 47
functional categories, 48-60
Communicative approach, fundamental postulates, 80-81
principles, 81-82
Communicative competence, 57, 70-72, 86, 119-20, 134-38, 176-78
functions, 86-87
specification, 107-08
Communicative curriculum, 53-55
Communicative events, characterisation of, 48-50
Communicative methodology, 73, 78-80, 82, 88-89
Communicative programme, categories of, 106
Communicative setting, 52

Communicative skill, development of, 65-67
Communicative terms, 43-45
  categories, 44-45
Communicative testing, issues in, 104-06
Compatriots, 13
Compulsory English courses, 53-55
Compulsory subjects, 23-25, 42-43
Confusion, 140
Context of situation, 130-31
Consequences, essential ingredient, 33
Constituent colleges, 177
Constraints, 26-27, 43, 46, 50, 172
Conventional English teaching, 29-50
Conventional language teaching method, 75
Conversation, 56
  function of, 36-37
  strategies and tactics, 74-75
Cook, V.J., 37, 39, 61
Cordes, S. Pit, 85
Core remedial grammar, 18
Correct behaviour, 88
Correct errors, 32, 82-83
Cultural organisation, 163
Curriculum, 42, 53-56
  planning, 33-35
Curriculum Development Centre, 41

Darbhanga, ESL teaching, problems of, 34-35
  inter-schools and colleges, 148-49
  nativisation of, 114-15, 125-35
  socio-linguistic regions, 20-21, 171-72
Das, Mohajiteswar, 35
Data analysis, 148-60
  collection of, 149-50
Davies English Proficiency Test, 102
Desired terminal behaviour, 62-63
Deviations, 119-20, 176-78
  type of, 144-45
Diphthongs, 136-37
Disciplines, 65
Discriminations, 99
Divergences, 115
Domains, 118, 121-22
Dominant language group, 20-21
Downward spiral, 31
Durant, Alen, 14, 15

Economic variables, 28-29
Edge, Julian, 28
Education, level of, 123-24
Education, policy-making design, 40-41
Education system, in-build problems in, 124-25
Educational domain, 161-62
Educational model, 82
Ellis, Rod, 71, 85
English, change status of, 30-31
  forms and functions of, 26
  honours courses, 54
  learning and teaching, 40-42
  pidgimised forms, 21
English Language Teaching (ELT), 18-19, 23-24
  problems of, 25-26
  programmes, 35
  qualitative change in, 23-24
  situation, 21-22
  socio-cultural aspects of, 114-40
  teaching/learning process of, 29-30
English medium schools, 22, 34
English movies, 29
English, nativisation of, 114-15
English pronunciation, tremendous variation in, 26
  variety of, 82
English Bilingualism, 121
English language tests, 103
English Textbooks, 58-59
Entrance Behaviour, 62
Error analysis, 115-16
Errors and mistakes, 119-20
ESL (English as a Second Language), 34-35, 116
Essay type questions, 98
Ethnic variations, 115-16
Exaggeration, 28
Examination system, 25-26
Examination/evaluation system, 22
Extra linguistic components, 31

Falling apart, 25
Fishman, J.A., 130
Fluency, 88-89
Foreign languages, 15, 72-73
  problematic areas, 31-32
  teaching, 51-52
French morphology, 37
Frequency counts, 59-60
Frustration, 78
Functional syllabus, 72

Functionalism, 78

General English course, objectives of, 158-59
Generalisation, 90-91
Good examination, requirements of, 98-110
Gopalkrishnan, G.S., 114
Government policy, 16-17
Grammar, rules of, 86
Grammar-based approach, 76
Grammar translation method, 50, 91-92
Grammatical accuracy, 172
Grammatical construction, 145
Grammatical errors, 81
Grammatical features, 20
Grammatical structures, 57-60
Grammatical syllabus, 79-80
Grammatical system, 50
Gujarati English, 114
Gumperz, J.J., 117, 118

Halliday, M.A.K., 74
Hardware equipments, 69
Harry, P., 114
Hatch, E., 39
Hindi, dialectical variation, 21, 40-42
Hyderabadi English, 114
Hymes, D., 116

Indian English, 82
  models, 14-15
  phonology, 19-20
  problem of interference in, 114
  varieties of, 15-16, 115-16
Information gap, 73
Intellectual linguistic message, 132-33
Intelligibility, 110
Interlingual grammar, 91
Intermediate Answer script, 194-95
Intermediate Question script, 182-93
Inter University Board, 42
Internal linguistic situation, 40
Intra-ethnic communication, 124

Jaggernaut, 29
Jakoboviti, Leon A., 70
Johnson, Keith, 72, 74

Kachru, B.B., 13, 14, 114, 115, 117, 118, 120, 143-45
Khubchandani, 123
Kitchen English, 115
Krashen, S.P., 77, 78
Kundu, M., 18, 111
Kunzru Committee, 16

Lal, B.K., 18, 139
Lalit Narayan Mithila University, 53
Languages, 14
  competence, 95-96
  features, 92
  preferences, 122-23
  proficiency, 31-36
  problems, 75-76, 129-30
  programme, 56
    testing system, 103-04
  shifts, 115-16
  system, 50-51
  training, 45
Language evaluation, 83-84, 91-95, 97-98
  testing procedures 109-12
Languages laboratory, samples of, 180-82
Language learning, encouragement and organisation, 41-42, 97
Language planning, 41, 175-76
  issues of, 171-72
Language teaching, 70-71, 79-80
  interim model, 90-91
  method, evaluation of, 83-84
  methodology, 70, 81-82
  modes of, 92-93
  non-segmental physiological features, 84
  objectives of, 75-76
  teaching materials of, 63-75
  techniques, 71-72, 97-98
Language testing, 91-95
  problems of, 103-04
  principles of, 92-95
  shift of emphasis in, 92-93
  techniques, 97-98
Latley, E., 39
Le Page, R.B., 70, 112, 142
Learning English, aims of, 155-56
Lewis, E.G., 91
Lexis, 143-47
Liberalisation, 37
Linguistic, application of, 174-75
  conventions, 172-73
  demands of, 41
  encoding, 49
  features, 68-69, 179-80

forms, 74-75
knowledge, 41
levels, 116-17
methods of, 91-92
performance, 95-96
dimensions of, 96-97
principles, 92-95
repertoire, 118-119, 172-73
syllabus, 52
Littlewood, William, 80, 81
Logical communication, categories of, 48-49
Lowerberg, Peter Harper, 14

Magdhi language, 40, 71, 161-62
Maithili language, 20-21
speech fellowship, 117-18
Maithili English 114
Mental conversion, 57
Mesolect, 126-27
Methodological framework, 26-27
Micro-functions, 49
Misconception, 88
Mishra, Arpita, 128, 129
Mistakes committed, 82
Mistaken haste, 38
Model question, 113
Morrow, K., 74
Mother tongue, 114
habits, 15
Motivation, 39-42
Mukherjee, Ranajit, 19
Munby, John 43, 46

National policy on education, 41
National syllabuses, 78-79
Native speaker varieties, 115
Nativisation, 114-15, 125-35
type of, 171-72
NCERT, 63
Negligence, 25
Negotiation, 86-88
Nepal, 20, 25
N.J. Mahila College, Laheriasarai, 22
Non-academic factors, 68-69
Non-conventional methods, 24-25
Non-linguistic devices, 31
factors, 68-69, 112-13
reasons, 164-68
syllabus, 52-53
Non-native language, 175-76
Non-segmental phonemes, 137-38

Observations, 140
Occupational language teaching, 45
O'Connor, J.D., 68
Official policy, 42
Old fogeyism, 38
Oral examination, 110
Orientation courses, 25
Oriya English, 114
Orthographic form, 136
Outworn teaching methodology, 22
Overgeneralism, 39

Palmer, Harold E., 32, 35, 36, 60, 77
Pan-Indian languages, 14, 16
Paralinguistic feature, 131-32
Parameters, 43, 46-48
Parashar, S.V., 18
Paruchuri, Usha Prasad, 20
Pass Without English (PWE), 23
Patnaik, B.N., 83
Pedagogic conditions, 169-70
Pedagogy, 47
Phonological data, 26
differences, 15
Pidgin languages, 39-40
Political interference, 30
Political variables, 128
Prabhu, N.S., 90
Pramanik, T.K., 19, 114
Prejudice, 38
Pride, J.B., 143
Primary sources, 26
Professions, usefulness of languages in, 123-24
Proficiency, 37-38, 41
Programme of action, 41
Pronunciation, 26-27, 45
Proportional curriculum, 51

Quality of teachers, 62
Quarrel of Hindi, 171
Questionnaires, 149-50
distribution of, 150
Quirk, Randolph, 13, 58

Ranjitha, J.A., 19, 84
Reading aloud, 96-97
Reading comprehension, 96-97
Reading materials, 155-56

Recurrent domain, 115
Regional languages, 17-18, 53-54, 114-15
Regional variations, 127-28
Regional strains, 14
Reliability, 99-100
Remedial measures, suggestions for, 171-78
Restricted domains, 22
Rivers, W.M., 75
Rustic languages, 167

Samastipur, 20
Saraswathi, V., 18
Satyagraha, 173
Sawhney, S.K., 18, 112
Second language, category of, 37-44
Secondary courses, 26
  patterning of, 53-55
Segmental phonemes, 135-36
Segmental stress, 92
Segregation, 36-37
Self-instruction courses, 36
Sen, Julu, 19
Shakespeare, 58
Sharma, A.K., 20, 140, 149, 160
Situational variables, 131
Slang expressions, 83
Social control, 48
Socio-cultural factors, 21
Socio-cultural variables, 111-12, 128-30, 133-34
Socio-linguistic factors, 18
Socio-semantic processing, 48-50
Software equipment, 89
Speak English, unacceptable varieties, 34
Speech community, 116-18
Speech fellowship, 116-18
Spelling errors, 144
  specimen of, 197-98
Steiner, F. 51.
Strategies, 39-40
Strevens, Peter, 44
Structural dialogues, 87
Structural item, 72
Structural words, 60-61
Students' attitude, 154-55
  behaviour, 33
  categories 35
  comprehension skill, 164-66
  cultural background, 36
  English conversion difficulties, 40
  enrolments of, 151-52
  father/guardian occupation of, 153-54, 160-61
  intelligence categories, 38
  language learning procedures, 34
  motivation, 162
  opting English, 150-51
  participation, 165-166
  socio-economic conditions, 149-50
  teaching schedule, 42
Students S.S.E. Board Examination, 183
Students and teachers, questionnaire of, 198-204
Sudhakar, G., 19
Subjective judgement, consistency, 100-101
Subsidiary sources, 54
Swami Vivekananda, 29
Swan, M., 86
Syllabuses, 23-25
  designers, 47, 63-65
  dimensions of, 43
  manifestation, 174
  planners, 78-80
  policy-making design, 40-41
Syllabus demands intensive teaching, 159-60
Syntex, 138-43
Synthetic language teaching strategy, 79

Tamil English, 114
Teaching aids, 55-62
Teaching comprehension skill, 87
Teaching English, 175-76
Teaching environment, 30
Teaching language, 168
Teaching/learning, deteriorating condition, 22, 26-27
  importance of teachers, 29-30
Teaching material, 24-25, 55-65, 67-68
  factors of, 62-63
  formal and informal styles, 58-59
  preparing of, 61-62
Teaching, methods/techniques, 24-25
  methodology, 69-90
  modern techniques, 31
Teachers, 29-32
  career of, 30
  functions of, 32
  performance of, 32-33
  opinions, 157
  physical factors, 32

Teacher-student relationship, 30
Technicalia, 148-49
Test procedure, 99-100
Testing techniques, 42
Teenagers, learning grammars, 37
Tickoo, M.L., 23
Thomas, C.J., 19
Traditional correlation procedures, 98
Traditional syllabus, 50
Transfer, type of, 146
Translation, 196
Transaction domain, 122
Tuition and coaching classes, 165
Tutorial classes, 178
T.V. advertisements, 30

UGC Project, 41
Uncontrolled exposures, 30
Undergraduate courses, syllabus of, 84
Unintelligibility, 172
Unstressed syllabus, vowels in, 15
Urdu, 21

Validity, 101-102
Vallette, Rebacca, 72
Variables, 25, 29-35
  focus, 51
Variance, sources of, 115
Vocabulary, 59, 60-62
Vowels, 7, 15, 36-37

Weinreich, U., 138
West, Michael, 61
Widdowson, H.G., 35, 56, 71, 86, 87
Wilkinson, D.A., 79
Words, type of, 59-60
Wong, Irene F.H., 115
World War I, 77

Yadav, Y.P. ,18, 19, 114
Yalden, Janice, 42, 43, 50, 51
Yule, George, 127